The Python Developer's Toolkit

Everything You Need to Go from Beginner to Pro in Web, Data, and Automation

Booker Blunt

Rafael Sanders

Miguel Farmer

Boozman Richard

Chapter 1: Introduction to Python – Getting Started........... 8

   Overview of Python 8

   Setting Up Your Development Environment 9

   Real-World Example: Customizing Your First Program 12

Chapter 2: Python Fundamentals – Syntax, Variables, and
Data Types... 15

   Introduction to Python Syntax 15

   Understanding Python Syntax 16

   Working with Variables and Data Types 17

   Simple Input and Output 19

   Hands-On Project: Building a Simple Calculator 21

Chapter 3: Control Flow – Loops, Conditionals, and
Functions 24

   What You'll Need 24

   Introduction to Control Flow in Python 24

   1. Mastering Loops in Python................................. 25

   2. Conditional Statements (if, elif, else) 28

   3. Defining and Using Functions 31

   Hands-On Project: Building a Simple Banking System 33

Chapter 4: Data Structures – Lists, Tuples, Dictionaries, and
Sets 36

   Introduction to Data Structures............................. 36

   1. Working with Lists 37

   2. Using Tuples and Sets..................................... 40

   Sets 41

   3. Mastering Dictionaries 42

4. When to Use Each Data Structure 44

Hands-On Project: Building a Contact Book 46

Chapter 5: Object-Oriented Programming (OOP) in Python
.... 48

Introduction to OOP Concepts 48

1. Creating Classes and Objects.. 49

2. Inheritance.. 51

3. Polymorphism 53

4. Encapsulation 54

Using Encapsulation 56

Hands-On Project: Building a Simple Banking System with
OOP 56

Chapter 6: Web Development with Flask........................ 59

Introduction to Flask... 60

Chapter 7: Data Science Basics – Pandas and NumPy...... 70

Introduction to Data Science 71

1. Data Manipulation with Pandas 71

2. Using NumPy for Numerical Computing............................ 76

3. Practical Project: Analyzing Sales Data............................ 79

Chapter 8: Data Visualization with Matplotlib 82

Understanding Data Visualization 83

Chapter 9: Automation with Python: Scripts for Everyday
Tasks.. 95

Introduction to Automation 96

1. Automating File Management 96

Practical Projects: Automating Daily Tasks......................... 104

Chapter 10: Interacting with APIs: Fetching Data from the
Web 108

Introduction to APIs and HTTP Requests 109

Chapter 11: Database Operations with SQL and Python ..118

Introduction to Databases and SQL 119

1. Working with SQLite 121

2. Executing Queries with Python 125

3. Connecting Python to Databases and Executing Queries 129

Chapter 12: Web Scraping: Extracting Data from Websites
....132

Introduction to Web Scraping 133

1. Basics of Web Scraping 133

2. Using BeautifulSoup and Requests 134

3. Scraping and Storing Data in CSV Files 138

4. Real-World Example: Scraping Product Data 140

Chapter 13: Machine Learning with Scikit-Learn 143

Introduction to Machine Learning Concepts 144

1. Implementing Linear Regression with Scikit-Learn 145

2. Evaluating Machine Learning Models 150

Chapter 14: Building a Python-Powered E-Commerce
Application 154

Introduction to Building E-Commerce Applications 155

1. Planning and Designing an E-Commerce Site 156

2. Integrating Front-End and Back-End with Flask 157

3. User Authentication and Database Management 162

4. Wrapping Up: E-Commerce Features 164

Chapter 15: Capstone Project: Building a Complete Python
Application 166

Introduction to the Capstone Project 167

2. Step-by-Step Project Development 168

3. Step-by-Step Project Development 173

4. Deploying Your Application 175

How to Scan a Barcode to Get a Repository

1. **Install a QR/Barcode Scanner** – Ensure you have a barcode or QR code scanner app installed on your smartphone or use a built-in scanner in **GitHub, GitLab, or Bitbucket.**

2. **Open the Scanner** – Launch the scanner app and grant necessary camera permissions.

3. **Scan the Barcode** – Align the barcode within the scanning frame. The scanner will automatically detect and process it.

4. **Follow the Link** – The scanned result will display a **URL to the repository**. Tap the link to open it in your web browser or Git client.

5. **Clone the Repository** – Use **Git clone** with the provided URL to download the repository to your local machine.

Chapter 1: Introduction to Python – Getting Started

Overview of Python

Python is one of the most popular and versatile programming languages in the world today. It's known for its simplicity, readability, and ease of use, which makes it an excellent choice for beginners. But don't let its user-friendly nature fool you; Python is a powerful tool that professionals use to build everything from simple websites to complex machine learning models.

Imagine you have a hammer, and you can use it to build anything from a small birdhouse to a full-scale house. Python is like that hammer for developers—it's flexible enough to tackle a wide range of projects.

Why Python?

- **Simple Syntax**: Python's syntax is easy to understand. You won't get bogged down by complex rules or unnecessarily long lines of code.

- **Highly Readable Code**: Python code looks almost like English, which makes it intuitive.

- **Versatility**: Python can be used for web development, automation, data analysis, artificial intelligence, and even robotics.

- **Large Community**: Python has a large, supportive community. There are tons of resources available, whether you're looking for help with a problem or building on your skills.

- **Cross-Platform Compatibility**: Python works across different platforms—Windows, macOS, and Linux—making it perfect for developers working on various systems.

Setting Up Your Development Environment

Before you start writing Python code, you need to set up your development environment. Don't worry; this step is easy! We'll go through it together.

What You'll Need

To begin programming with Python, you'll need the following:

1. **A Computer**: Python runs on most computers, so whether you're using a Mac, Windows, or Linux machine, you're all set. If you're working on a computer, make sure it has at least 2GB of RAM, though 4GB is preferred.

2. **Python Installed**: You can download Python from its official website: python.org. Most operating systems come with Python pre-installed, but it's always a good idea to check if you have the latest version.

   o **Windows Users**: When installing Python on Windows, ensure you check the box that says "Add Python to PATH." This step will make sure you can run Python from the command line.

   o **Mac/Linux Users**: Python usually comes pre-installed, but it's good practice to install the latest version using Homebrew on Mac or the package manager on Linux (apt, yum, etc.).

3. **Text Editor or Integrated Development Environment (IDE)**: You'll need somewhere to write your code. While you can use any text editor (like Notepad on Windows), a dedicated Python IDE or code editor will provide better features like syntax highlighting and error checking. Some popular options are:

   o   **PyCharm** (Advanced)

   o   **VS Code** (Beginner to Advanced)

   o   **Sublime Text** (Beginner to Advanced)

   o   **Jupyter Notebook** (For Data Science)

You can download and install any of these editors based on your preferences. For beginners, I recommend **VS Code** because it's lightweight and beginner-friendly.

4. **Command Line or Terminal**: You'll also need to open a command-line interface (CLI) to run your Python scripts. The terminal (macOS/Linux) or command prompt (Windows) is where you can execute your code.

Your First Python Program

Now that your environment is set up, it's time for your first Python program! We'll write a simple Python script that prints the words "Hello, World!" to the screen. This is traditionally the first program that many new developers write.

Step 1: Create Your Python Script

1. Open your text editor or IDE (for this example, we'll use VS Code).

2. Create a new file and name it hello.py. The .py extension is used for Python scripts.

In the file, type the following code:

python

 # This is a simple Python program that prints "Hello, World!"

print("Hello, World!")

Step 2: Run Your Python Script

- **Windows**:

    1. Open Command Prompt (press Windows + R, then type cmd and hit Enter).

    2. Navigate to the folder where you saved your hello.py file using the cd command. For example:

bash

cd C:\Users\YourName\Desktop

    3. Run the script by typing:

bash

python hello.py

- **Mac/Linux**:

    1. Open Terminal.

    2. Navigate to the folder where your hello.py file is saved using the cd command:

bash

```
cd ~/Desktop
```

3. Run the script by typing:

```bash
```

```
python3 hello.py
```

Step 3: See the Output

Once you run the script, you should see the following output:

```
Hello, World!
```

Congratulations, you've just written and executed your first Python program! You've learned how to:

- Create a Python script.

- Write a simple Python statement to output text.

- Run your Python script from the command line.

Real-World Example: Customizing Your First Program

To make your first program more interactive, let's modify it to ask for the user's name and print a personalized greeting. Here's an updated version of the program:

```python
```

```
# This program asks for the user's name and prints a greeting
```

```
# Asking for user's name
name = input("What is your name? ")

# Printing a personalized greeting
print("Hello, " + name + "! Welcome to Python.")
```

How It Works:

1. **input()**: This function asks the user to input something through the command line. The text inside the parentheses is the prompt that the user will see.

2. **print()**: This function prints the greeting message to the screen. The + operator is used to combine (concatenate) strings.

Step 1: Save and Run the Program

Follow the same steps to save this updated script as greeting.py and run it. When you run it, you should see something like this:

```
pgsql
```

```
What is your name? Alice
Hello, Alice! Welcome to Python.
```

This program demonstrates how you can make interactive Python applications. By learning how to use functions like input(), you'll be able to build more complex and engaging programs!

Key Takeaways

1. **Python is easy to learn and versatile**: Whether you want to build websites, analyze data, or automate tasks, Python has tools and libraries for it.

2. **Setting up your environment is simple**: With Python and a text editor, you can start coding in no time.

3. **You've written your first Python program!**: Not only have you written your first script, but you've also customized it to interact with the user. This is just the beginning!

What's Next?

In the next chapters, we'll dive deeper into Python's capabilities. We'll explore key concepts like data types, variables, loops, and functions—building on the foundation you've just created.

Keep going, and remember: The more you practice, the more you'll get comfortable with Python!

Chapter 2: Python Fundamentals – Syntax, Variables, and Data Types

Introduction to Python Syntax

Before we dive into the deeper aspects of Python programming, it's essential to understand the building blocks that make up Python syntax. Python is often praised for its clean and readable syntax, making it one of the easiest programming languages to learn. You'll notice that Python code almost looks like simple English, which makes it incredibly beginner-friendly.

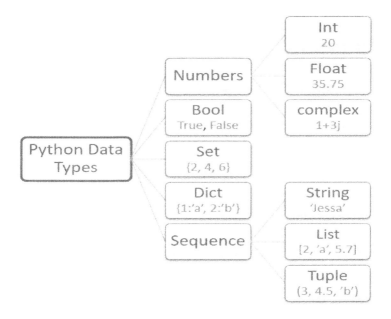

Before we begin, let's review the software and hardware setup required:

- **A Computer**: This guide will work on any machine—Windows, macOS, or Linux.

- **Python Installation**: If you haven't already, make sure Python is installed on your system. You can download it from python.org.

- **Text Editor or IDE**: I recommend using **VS Code** or **Sublime Text** for your Python code. If you're doing data science or working with Jupyter Notebooks, you may prefer **Jupyter** or **PyCharm**.

- **Command Line Access**: On Windows, use Command Prompt; on Mac/Linux, use the Terminal.

Understanding Python Syntax

At the core of any programming language is its syntax—the rules that define how you write code. In Python, the syntax is designed to be simple and human-readable, so you don't have to deal with a lot of complicated symbols or punctuation.

1. Comments in Python

Comments are a critical part of writing clear code. They are lines of text in your code that Python ignores when running the program. Comments help you explain what your code does, which is useful for anyone reading your code, including your future self.

In Python, a comment begins with a # symbol:

python

```
# This is a single-line comment
print("Hello, World!")  # This prints "Hello, World!"
```

2. Indentation in Python

Unlike many programming languages that use braces {} to define blocks of code, Python uses **indentation** (spaces or tabs) to structure the code. The indentation tells Python which lines of code belong to a specific block.

For example, in a loop or function, the indented lines will be considered part of that block:

```python
if True:
    print("This is inside the if statement")
```

Incorrect indentation will result in an error:

```python
if True:
print("This will cause an error due to wrong indentation")
```

Python is very strict about indentation, so it's essential to keep your code properly aligned.

Working with Variables and Data Types

What Are Variables?

Variables in Python are used to store data that your program can use. You can think of variables as containers or storage boxes that hold a value. Once a variable is assigned a value, you can use that value throughout your program.

To create a variable in Python, simply assign a value to it using the = operator:

python

```
# Assigning a value to a variable
name = "John"
age = 25
```

In the above example:

- name is a variable that holds a string ("John").

- age is a variable that holds an integer (25).

Data Types in Python

Python supports various data types, and understanding them is fundamental to working with the language. Here's a breakdown of the most common data types in Python:

- **Integers (int):** Whole numbers, positive or negative, without a decimal point.

python

```
age = 25  # Integer
```

- **Floating-point numbers (float):** Numbers that contain a decimal point.

python

```
height = 5.8  # Float
```

- **Strings (str):** A sequence of characters enclosed in single or double quotes.

```python
```

```python
name = "Alice"  # String
```

- **Booleans (bool)**: Represents True or False values.

```python
is_adult = True  # Boolean
```

- **Lists (list)**: Ordered collections that can hold any data type.

```python
colors = ["red", "green", "blue"]  # List
```

- **Dictionaries (dict)**: A collection of key-value pairs.

```python
person = {"name": "John", "age": 25}  # Dictionary
```

Simple Input and Output

In Python, interacting with the user is easy. You can take input from the user and display output to the user.

1. Taking User Input

To get input from a user, Python provides the input() function. This function pauses the program and waits for the user to type something.

Example of getting the user's name:

```python
name = input("What is your name? ")
print("Hello, " + name + "!")
```

In the above code:

- input() displays a prompt and waits for the user to type something.

- The value entered by the user is stored in the name variable.

- print() outputs the string to the console.

2. Converting Input Data Types

By default, the input() function always returns a string, even if the user types a number. If you need to perform arithmetic or other operations, you might want to convert the input into a different data type (e.g., integer or float).

Here's how you can convert the input into an integer:

```python
age = input("Enter your age: ")
age = int(age)  # Convert input to integer
print("Next year, you will be " + str(age + 1) + " years old.")
```

In this example, int() is used to convert the input string to an integer so that we can perform arithmetic operations.

Hands-On Project: Building a Simple Calculator

Let's put what we've learned so far into practice by building a simple calculator that adds, subtracts, multiplies, and divides two numbers. This project will use variables, basic arithmetic operations, user input, and conditional statements.

Step 1: Taking User Input

First, we'll ask the user to input two numbers. We'll also ask them to choose an operation.

```python
# Get the numbers and the operation from the user
num1 = float(input("Enter the first number: "))
num2 = float(input("Enter the second number: "))
operation = input("Choose an operation (+, -, *, /): ")
```

Step 2: Perform the Calculation

Based on the user's choice, we will perform the corresponding operation.

```python
# Perform the calculation based on the chosen operation
if operation == "+":
    result = num1 + num2
elif operation == "-":
    result = num1 - num2
elif operation == "*":
```

```python
    result = num1 * num2
elif operation == "/":
    result = num1 / num2
else:
    result = "Invalid operation"
```

Step 3: Output the Result

Finally, we will display the result to the user.

```python

# Display the result
print("The result is: " + str(result))
```

Full Calculator Program:

```python

# Simple Python Calculator
num1 = float(input("Enter the first number: "))
num2 = float(input("Enter the second number: "))
operation = input("Choose an operation (+, -, *, /): ")

if operation == "+":
    result = num1 + num2
elif operation == "-":
    result = num1 - num2
elif operation == "*":
    result = num1 * num2
elif operation == "/":
    result = num1 / num2
```

```
else:
    result = "Invalid operation"

print("The result is: " + str(result))
```

Key Takeaways from This Chapter

- **Python Syntax** is clean and readable, using indentation to define code blocks and comments for clarity.

- **Variables** store data in Python. Variables can hold data of various types like integers, floats, strings, and more.

- **Data Types** include integers, floats, strings, booleans, lists, and dictionaries, each serving a specific purpose in your programs.

- **Input and Output**: The input() function allows you to interact with the user, while print() helps display results.

- **Practical Examples**: We built a simple calculator as an example project that demonstrates how to work with variables, data types, user input, and conditional statements.

Chapter 3: Control Flow – Loops, Conditionals, and Functions

What You'll Need

Before we jump into the code, let's ensure you have everything you need:

- **A Computer**: Whether you're using a Windows, Mac, or Linux system, Python will work across all platforms.

- **Python Installation**: Make sure Python is installed. You can download the latest version from python.org.

- **Text Editor or IDE**: I recommend using **VS Code**, **PyCharm**, or **Sublime Text**. If you're doing data-related tasks, **Jupyter** or **Spyder** can be good choices.

- **Command Line or Terminal**: You'll need a command-line interface (CLI) to run your Python scripts. On Windows, that's Command Prompt or PowerShell; on Mac/Linux, use the Terminal.

Introduction to Control Flow in Python

Control flow is a crucial concept in any programming language. It determines the **order in which the code runs**. Control flow allows you to:

1. Make decisions in your program using **conditional statements**.

2. Repeat actions using **loops**.

3. Organize your code with **functions**.

By mastering these concepts, you can write more efficient, dynamic, and interactive programs.

---

1. Mastering Loops in Python

Loops are powerful tools in Python that allow us to repeat actions multiple times. There are two primary types of loops in Python: the for loop and the while loop. Let's take a look at both.

For Loop

The for loop is used to iterate over a sequence (such as a list, tuple, or string) and execute a block of code for each element.

Syntax:

```python

for variable in sequence:
    # Code to execute
```

Example 1: Printing Items in a List

Let's say you have a list of fruits, and you want to print each fruit one by one:

```python

fruits = ["apple", "banana", "cherry", "date"]
```

```
for fruit in fruits:
    print(fruit)
```

Explanation:

- fruits is a list.

- The for loop goes through each item in the fruits list, and the variable fruit holds the current item for each iteration.

- print(fruit) prints each item in the list.

Example 2: Using range() in a For Loop

The range() function allows you to generate a sequence of numbers. You can use it to run a loop a specific number of times.

```python
```

```
for i in range(5):  # Loop will run 5 times (0 to 4)
    print(i)
```

Explanation:

- range(5) generates numbers from 0 to 4.

- The loop runs 5 times, printing each number.

While Loop

The while loop continues to execute a block of code as long as the specified condition is True.

Syntax:

```python
```

```
while condition:
    # Code to execute
```

Example 1: Counting with While Loop

Let's write a program to count from 1 to 5 using a while loop.

```python
count = 1

while count <= 5:
    print(count)
    count += 1  # Increment count by 1
```

Explanation:

- The loop will run as long as count <= 5.

- After each iteration, count is incremented by 1 using count += 1.

Example 2: While Loop with User Input

Let's create a program that asks for the user's name repeatedly until they enter "exit".

```python
while True:
    name = input("Enter your name (or type 'exit' to quit): ")
```

```
if name == "exit":
    break  # Exit the loop if the user types "exit"
print("Hello, " + name + "!")
```

Explanation:

- The loop runs indefinitely due to while True.

- The program checks if the user typed "exit". If so, it breaks out of the loop.

---

2. Conditional Statements (if, elif, else)

Conditional statements allow you to execute code based on specific conditions. This makes your program dynamic and capable of making decisions.

If Statement

The if statement is used to check if a condition is True. If the condition evaluates to True, the code inside the if block runs.

Syntax:

```python
if condition:
    # Code to execute if condition is True
```

Example 1: Checking If a Number is Positive or Negative

```python
num = int(input("Enter a number: "))

if num > 0:
```

```
    print("The number is positive.")
```

Explanation:

- The program checks if the number is greater than 0.

- If True, it prints "The number is positive."

Elif (Else If)

If the condition in an if statement is False, you can use the elif statement to check additional conditions.

Syntax:

```python
if condition1:
    # Code for condition1
elif condition2:
    # Code for condition2
Example 2: Checking Multiple Conditions
python

num = int(input("Enter a number: "))

if num > 0:
    print("The number is positive.")
elif num < 0:
    print("The number is negative.")
else:
    print("The number is zero.")
```

Explanation:

- The program first checks if the number is positive. If not, it checks if the number is negative. If both conditions are False, it prints "The number is zero."

Else Statement

The else statement runs if all previous conditions are False.

Example 3: Making a Simple Grade Checker

```python
score = int(input("Enter your score (0-100): "))

if score >= 90:
    print("Grade: A")
elif score >= 80:
    print("Grade: B")
elif score >= 70:
    print("Grade: C")
elif score >= 60:
    print("Grade: D")
else:
    print("Grade: F")
```

Explanation:

- The program assigns grades based on the score entered by the user.

3. Defining and Using Functions

Functions are reusable blocks of code that perform a specific task. Using functions helps keep your code organized, readable, and easy to maintain.

Defining a Function

To define a function in Python, you use the def keyword, followed by the function name, parentheses, and a colon.

Syntax:

```python
def function_name(parameters):
    # Code to execute
```

Example 1: A Simple Function

```python
def greet():
    print("Hello, welcome to Python programming!")

greet()  # Calling the function
```

Explanation:

- The function greet() prints a greeting when called.

- The parentheses () can be empty if the function doesn't require parameters.

Functions with Parameters

Functions can also accept **parameters**—values you pass to the function to modify its behavior.

Example 2: Function with Parameters

```python
def greet(name):
    print("Hello, " + name + "! Welcome to Python.")

greet("Alice")  # Passing a parameter to the function
```

Explanation:

- The greet() function now accepts a name parameter and prints a personalized message.

- When we call greet("Alice"), it prints "Hello, Alice! Welcome to Python."

Returning Values from Functions

Functions can return values using the return statement. This allows you to use the result of the function in other parts of your code.

Example 3: Function Returning a Value

```python
def add_numbers(a, b):
    return a + b

result = add_numbers(3, 5)
print("The sum is:", result)
```

Explanation:

- The add_numbers() function takes two parameters and returns their sum.

- The result is stored in the variable result and printed.

Hands-On Project: Building a Simple Banking System

Let's combine what we've learned in this chapter to create a simple banking system. This system will allow users to deposit and withdraw money, check their balance, and exit the program.

Step 1: Define Functions for Each Action

We'll create functions for depositing money, withdrawing money, and checking the balance.

```python
balance = 0

def deposit(amount):
    global balance
    balance += amount
    print(f"Deposited: ${amount}. New balance: ${balance}")

def withdraw(amount):
    global balance
    if amount > balance:
        print("Insufficient funds!")
    else:
        balance -= amount
        print(f"Withdrew: ${amount}. New balance: ${balance}")
```

```python
def check_balance():
    print(f"Your balance is: ${balance}")
```

Step 2: Create the Menu and Input Loop

Now, let's create a menu where the user can choose an action.

```python
while True:
    print("\nBanking System Menu:")
    print("1. Deposit")
    print("2. Withdraw")
    print("3. Check Balance")
    print("4. Exit")

    choice = input("Enter your choice (1/2/3/4): ")

    if choice == "1":
        amount = float(input("Enter amount to deposit: "))
        deposit(amount)
    elif choice == "2":
        amount = float(input("Enter amount to withdraw: "))
        withdraw(amount)
    elif choice == "3":
        check_balance()
    elif choice == "4":
        print("Thank you for using the banking system. Goodbye!")
        break
    else:
        print("Invalid choice. Please try again.")
```

- **Loops**: for and while loops are powerful tools to repeat actions in Python.

- **Conditional Statements**: Use if, elif, and else to make decisions in your program.

- **Functions**: Functions allow you to reuse code, make your program more readable, and return results when needed.

Chapter 4: Data Structures – Lists, Tuples, Dictionaries, and Sets

Before we dive into the specifics of data structures, let's make sure you have everything you need to follow along:

- **A Computer**: Python works on all major operating systems (Windows, macOS, Linux).

- **Python Installation**: If you haven't already, download Python from python.org and ensure it's installed on your system.

- **Text Editor or IDE**: Any text editor will work, but I recommend using **VS Code**, **PyCharm**, or **Sublime Text** for a better coding experience.

- **Command Line or Terminal**: You'll need this to run your Python scripts. On Windows, you can use Command Prompt or PowerShell; on macOS/Linux, use the Terminal.

Introduction to Data Structures

In any programming language, **data structures** are ways of organizing and storing data efficiently. Python provides several built-in data structures, and mastering these will help you write more organized and efficient programs. In this chapter, we'll explore four of the most commonly used data structures:

1. **Tuples**

2. **Dictionaries**

3. **Sets**

Each data structure has its unique properties, advantages, and use cases, and we'll cover them with plenty of hands-on examples.

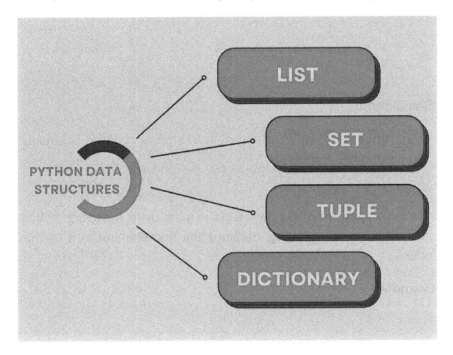

1. Working with Lists

A **list** is an ordered collection of elements that can hold items of different data types (such as integers, strings, or other lists). Lists are **mutable**, meaning you can change their content after they are created. They are one of the most versatile and commonly used data structures in Python.

Creating a List

To create a list, you simply enclose a sequence of values in square brackets [] and separate them with commas.

Example:

```python

fruits = ["apple", "banana", "cherry", "date"]
print(fruits)
```

Explanation:

- fruits is a list containing four strings: "apple", "banana", "cherry", and "date".

Accessing List Elements

You can access individual elements in a list using **indexing**. Python uses **zero-based indexing**, meaning the first element in a list has index 0.

Example:

```python

print(fruits[0])  # Output: apple
print(fruits[2])  # Output: cherry
```

Explanation:

- fruits[0] accesses the first item in the list, "apple".

- fruits[2] accesses the third item in the list, "cherry".

Modifying List Elements

Since lists are **mutable**, you can change an element by assigning a new value to an index.

Example:

```python
fruits[1] = "blueberry"
print(fruits)  # Output: ['apple', 'blueberry', 'cherry', 'date']
```

Explanation:

- fruits[1] = "blueberry" changes the second element (index 1) from "banana" to "blueberry".

Adding Items to a List

You can add elements to a list using the append() method, which adds an item to the end of the list.

Example:

```python
fruits.append("elderberry")
print(fruits)  # Output: ['apple', 'blueberry', 'cherry', 'date', 'elderberry']
```

Explanation:

- fruits.append("elderberry") adds "elderberry" to the end of the list.

Removing Items from a List

You can remove an element from a list using the remove() method, or you can pop an element at a specific index using the pop() method.

Example:

```python

fruits.remove("cherry")  # Removes the first occurrence of "cherry"
print(fruits)  # Output: ['apple', 'blueberry', 'date', 'elderberry']

popped_item = fruits.pop(2)  # Removes the item at index 2 (date)
print(popped_item)  # Output: date
print(fruits)  # Output: ['apple', 'blueberry', 'elderberry']
```

---

2. Using Tuples and Sets

Tuples

A **tuple** is similar to a list in that it can hold multiple elements, but **tuples are immutable**. Once a tuple is created, its contents cannot be modified. Tuples are typically used when you want to store data that shouldn't be changed after it's created.

Creating a Tuple

Tuples are created by enclosing values in parentheses ().

Example:

```python

coordinates = (10, 20, 30)
print(coordinates)
```

Explanation:

- coordinates is a tuple containing three integers.

Accessing Tuple Elements

Just like lists, you can access tuple elements using indexing.

Example:

```python
print(coordinates[0])  # Output: 10
print(coordinates[1])  # Output: 20
```

Why Use Tuples?

Tuples are typically used for storing **immutable** data that you want to ensure doesn't change. They are also **faster** than lists for certain operations because they are immutable.

Sets

A **set** is an unordered collection of unique items. Sets don't allow duplicates, and the order of elements in a set is not guaranteed.

Creating a Set

To create a set, you enclose the elements in curly braces {}.

Example:

```python
colors = ["red", "green", "blue"]
```

```
print(colors)
```

Explanation:

- colors is a set containing three strings: "red", "green", and "blue".

Adding and Removing Elements from a Set

You can add elements to a set using the add() method and remove them using the remove() or discard() methods.

Example:

```python
colors.add("yellow")  # Adds "yellow" to the set
print(colors)  # Output: {'blue', 'green', 'red', 'yellow'}

colors.remove("red")  # Removes "red" from the set
print(colors)  # Output: {'blue', 'green', 'yellow'}
```

Why Use Sets?

Sets are ideal when you need to store unique items and don't care about the order. They are also useful for performing mathematical set operations like union, intersection, and difference.

---

3. Mastering Dictionaries

A **dictionary** is an unordered collection of **key-value pairs**. Each key in a dictionary must be unique, and you can use keys to look up corresponding values.

Creating a Dictionary

Dictionaries are created using curly braces {} with key-value pairs separated by colons.

Example:

```python
python

person = {"name": "John", "age": 30, "city": "New York"}
print(person)
```

Explanation:

- person is a dictionary with three key-value pairs: "name": "John", "age": 30, and "city": "New York".

Accessing Values in a Dictionary

You can access the values in a dictionary using their corresponding keys.

Example:

```python
python

print(person["name"])  # Output: John
print(person["age"])   # Output: 30
```

Adding and Modifying Dictionary Entries

You can add new key-value pairs or modify existing ones by simply assigning a value to a key.

Example:

```python
python
```

```python
person["email"] = "john@example.com"  # Adds a new key-value pair

print(person)  # Output: {'name': 'John', 'age': 30, 'city': 'New York', 'email': 'john@example.com'}


person["age"] = 31  # Modifies the existing value for the key "age"

print(person)  # Output: {'name': 'John', 'age': 31, 'city': 'New York', 'email': 'john@example.com'}
```

Removing Items from a Dictionary

You can remove key-value pairs from a dictionary using the del statement or the pop() method.

Example:

```python
python


del person["city"]  # Removes the key "city"

print(person)  # Output: {'name': 'John', 'age': 31, 'email': 'john@example.com'}


email = person.pop("email")  # Removes the "email" key and returns the value

print(email)  # Output: john@example.com

print(person)  # Output: {'name': 'John', 'age': 31}
```

---

4. When to Use Each Data Structure

Choosing the right data structure is essential for writing efficient code. Here's a quick guide to help you decide which structure to use based on your needs:

Use a List:

- o   When you need an **ordered** collection of items.

- When you may need to **modify** the collection (add, remove, update).

- When the collection might contain **duplicates**.

Use a Tuple:

- When you need an **ordered** collection of items that should not be changed (immutable).

- When you need faster access to elements compared to lists.

- When you want to **protect** the data from accidental changes.

Use a Set:

- When you need a **collection of unique items** and don't care about order.

- When you need to perform **set operations** like union, intersection, and difference.

- When you want faster lookups and don't mind losing the order.

Use a Dictionary:

- When you need to associate **keys with values** (key-value pairs).

- When you need fast **lookups** by a unique key.

- When you want to easily **modify** or **add** key-value pairs.

Hands-On Project: Building a Contact Book

Let's apply what we've learned by building a **contact book**. This project will involve using lists, dictionaries, and sets to organize and manage contacts.

Step 1: Create a Dictionary of Contacts

We'll use a dictionary to store contacts where each contact's name is a key, and their phone number is the value.

python

```
contacts = {
    "Alice": "123-456-7890",
    "Bob": "987-654-3210",
    "Charlie": "555-555-5555"
}
```

Step 2: Adding a New Contact

We'll create a function to add a new contact.

python

```
def add_contact(name, phone_number):
    contacts[name] = phone_number
    print(f"Added {name} with phone number {phone_number}")

add_contact("David", "222-333-4444")
```

Step 3: Display All Contacts

We'll use a loop to display all contacts.

python

```
def display_contacts():
    for name, phone_number in contacts.items():
        print(f"{name}: {phone_number}")

display_contacts()
```

Key Takeaways

- **Lists** are ordered, mutable collections perfect for holding multiple items.

- **Tuples** are ordered, immutable collections useful when data should not change.

- **Sets** are unordered collections of unique items ideal for performing set operations.

- **Dictionaries** store key-value pairs and are great for fast lookups by keys.

Chapter 5: Object-Oriented Programming (OOP) in Python

Before diving into Object-Oriented Programming (OOP) concepts, let's ensure you have everything you need:

- **A Computer**: Python runs on all major operating systems, including Windows, macOS, and Linux.

- **Python Installation**: If you haven't already, download the latest version of Python from python.org.

- **Text Editor or IDE**: Any text editor will work, but I recommend **VS Code** or **PyCharm** for a more professional coding experience.

- **Command Line or Terminal**: You'll need this to run Python scripts on your machine. On Windows, you can use Command Prompt or PowerShell, and on macOS/Linux, use the Terminal.

With your setup in place, we can now explore Object-Oriented Programming (OOP) in Python.

Introduction to OOP Concepts

Object-Oriented Programming (OOP) is a programming paradigm that uses "objects" to represent data and methods to manipulate that data. It's one of the most widely used programming methodologies and is foundational for building large-scale applications in Python and many other languages.

The basic principles of OOP revolve around four key concepts:

1. **Classes and Objects**

2. **Inheritance**

3. **Polymorphism**

4. **Encapsulation**

Each of these principles helps organize your code in a way that is modular, scalable, and easier to maintain. Let's break these down one by one, starting with **Classes and Objects**.

---

1. Creating Classes and Objects

In OOP, a **class** is like a blueprint, and an **object** is an instance of that class. A class defines the properties and behaviors (also known as **attributes** and **methods**) that its objects will have.

Creating a Class

To create a class in Python, we use the class keyword followed by the class name and a colon. By convention, class names use **Pascal case** (capitalized words without spaces), such as Car, Person, or Animal.

Example:

```python

class Car:
    # Constructor to initialize attributes
```

```python
def __init__(self, make, model, year):
    self.make = make
    self.model = model
    self.year = year

    # Method to display car details
    def display_info(self):
        print(f"{self.year} {self.make} {self.model}")
```

Explanation:

- The __init__ method is called when a new object (instance) of the class is created. It initializes the object's attributes.

- self refers to the instance of the class itself.

- The display_info method is a function that belongs to the class and prints the details of the car.

Creating Objects from a Class

Once a class is defined, you can create **objects** from it. An object is an instance of a class, and you can create as many objects as you want from the same class.

Example:

```python
python

my_car = Car("Toyota", "Corolla", 2020)
my_car.display_info()  # Output: 2020 Toyota Corolla
```

Explanation:

- my_car is an object created from the Car class.

- We pass the make, model, and year as arguments when creating the object.

- The display_info method is called on the my_car object to display its details.

---

2. Inheritance

Inheritance allows one class to inherit the attributes and methods of another class. This helps avoid code duplication and promotes code reuse.

In Python, inheritance is achieved by passing the parent class as an argument to the child class when defining it.

Example:

```python
# Parent Class
class Vehicle:
    def __init__(self, make, model):
        self.make = make
        self.model = model

    def display_info(self):
        print(f"{self.make} {self.model}")

# Child Class (inherits from Vehicle)
class Car(Vehicle):
    def __init__(self, make, model, year):
        super().__init__(make, model)  # Calls the parent class constructor
```

```
self.year = year

def display_info(self):
    print(f"{self.year} {self.make} {self.model}")
```

Explanation:

- The Car class inherits from the Vehicle class.

- The super().__init__(make, model) line calls the constructor of the parent class (Vehicle) to initialize the make and model attributes.

- The Car class overrides the display_info method to add the year attribute.

Using Inherited Classes

You can create objects of the child class just like the parent class, and they will have all the attributes and methods of the parent class.

Example:

```python
my_car = Car("Toyota", "Corolla", 2020)
my_car.display_info() # Output: 2020 Toyota Corolla
```

Explanation:

- The my_car object is created from the Car class, which inherits from Vehicle.

- Even though Car overrides the display_info method, it still inherits the make and model attributes from Vehicle.

3. Polymorphism

Polymorphism allows different classes to implement methods that have the same name but behave differently. It enables you to use a unified interface for different objects.

In Python, polymorphism is often used with method overriding. When a subclass provides a specific implementation of a method that is already defined in the parent class, it is called **method overriding**.

Example:

```python
python

class Animal:
    def speak(self):
        print("Animal speaks")

class Dog(Animal):
    def speak(self):
        print("Woof!")

class Cat(Animal):
    def speak(self):
        print("Meow!")

# Polymorphism in action
animals = [Dog(), Cat()]

for animal in animals:
    animal.speak()
```

Explanation:

- The Dog and Cat classes override the speak method from the Animal class.

- We create a list of animals (animals = [Dog(), Cat()]) and iterate over it, calling the speak() method.

- Even though the speak method has the same name, it behaves differently for Dog and Cat objects.

Why Use Polymorphism?

Polymorphism allows you to treat different objects the same way while providing the flexibility to define specific behaviors for each type. It simplifies the code and improves maintainability.

---

4. Encapsulation

Encapsulation is the concept of bundling the data (attributes) and methods (functions) that operate on the data within a single unit (i.e., a class). It also involves restricting access to some of the object's attributes to prevent accidental modification. This is done using **access modifiers**.

In Python, we can use **private** and **public** attributes to control access to class members.

- **Public attributes**: Can be accessed directly from outside the class.

- **Private attributes**: Can only be accessed within the class. In Python, private attributes are denoted by a leading underscore (_) or double underscore (__).

Example:

python

54

```python
class BankAccount:
    def __init__(self, owner, balance=0):
        self.owner = owner
        self.__balance = balance  # Private attribute

    def deposit(self, amount):
        if amount > 0:
            self.__balance += amount
            print(f"Deposited ${amount}. New balance: ${self.__balance}")

    def withdraw(self, amount):
        if 0 < amount <= self.__balance:
            self.__balance -= amount
            print(f"Withdrew ${amount}. New balance: ${self.__balance}")
        else:
            print("Insufficient funds or invalid withdrawal amount.")

    def get_balance(self):
        return self.__balance  # Getter for private attribute
```

Explanation:

- The __balance attribute is private, meaning it cannot be accessed directly from outside the class.

- The deposit and withdraw methods are used to modify the balance.

- The get_balance method is a **getter** method that allows access to the private attribute.

Using Encapsulation

You can use the class as follows:

```python
account = BankAccount("John Doe")
account.deposit(1000)
account.withdraw(500)
print(account.get_balance())  # Output: 500
```

Explanation:

- The private __balance attribute is encapsulated, and all access to it is done through methods (deposit, withdraw, and get_balance).

Hands-On Project: Building a Simple Banking System with OOP

Let's combine everything we've learned about OOP into a simple banking system that manages multiple accounts. We will create classes for Account and Transaction, and use inheritance, polymorphism, and encapsulation to build the system.

Step 1: Create the Base Account Class

```python
class Account:
    def __init__(self, owner, balance=0):
        self.owner = owner
        self.__balance = balance
```

```python
def deposit(self, amount):
    if amount > 0:
        self.__balance += amount
        print(f"Deposited ${amount}. New balance: ${self.__balance}")

def withdraw(self, amount):
    if 0 < amount <= self.__balance:
        self.__balance -= amount
        print(f"Withdrew ${amount}. New balance: ${self.__balance}")
    else:
        print("Insufficient funds or invalid withdrawal amount.")

def get_balance(self):
    return self.__balance
```

Step 2: Create a Transaction Class for Specific Transaction Types

python

```python
class Transaction(Account):
    def __init__(self, owner, balance=0, transaction_type="Deposit"):
        super().__init__(owner, balance)
        self.transaction_type = transaction_type

    def record_transaction(self, amount):
        if self.transaction_type == "Deposit":
            self.deposit(amount)
        elif self.transaction_type == "Withdraw":
            self.withdraw(amount)
        print(f"Transaction: {self.transaction_type} of ${amount}")
```

Step 3: Testing the Banking System

```python
acc = Transaction("John Doe")
acc.record_transaction(1000)  # Deposit
acc.record_transaction(500)   # Withdraw
```

Key Takeaways

- **Classes and Objects** are the foundation of OOP, allowing you to organize and structure your code.

- **Inheritance** enables you to reuse code and extend functionality in subclasses.

- **Polymorphism** provides flexibility in your program by allowing methods with the same name to behave differently.

- **Encapsulation** protects the internal state of an object and provides controlled access through methods.

What's Next?

In the next chapter, we will dive into **exception handling** in Python—how to handle errors and create robust programs that can deal with unexpected situations.

Chapter 6: Web Development with Flask

Before you start building web applications with Flask, let's ensure you have everything set up and ready to go:

1. **A Computer**: Flask is cross-platform, so it will run on Windows, macOS, and Linux.

2. **Python Installed**: You need Python 3.x installed on your machine. You can download the latest version from python.org.

3. **Text Editor or IDE**: Use **VS Code**, **Sublime Text**, or **PyCharm** for a better coding experience. You can also use a lightweight text editor like **Notepad++** if you're just starting.

4. **Command Line or Terminal**: You'll need this to run your Python scripts. On Windows, use **Command Prompt** or **PowerShell**, and on macOS/Linux, use **Terminal**.

5. **Flask Installation**: Flask is a lightweight web framework for Python. You'll need to install it using **pip**, Python's package installer.

To install Flask, open your terminal/command prompt and type the following:

```bash
pip install flask
```

Once installed, you're ready to begin developing with Flask!

Introduction to Flask

Flask is a **micro-framework** for web development in Python. It is called a **micro-framework** because it provides the basic tools needed to build web applications, but it is minimalistic—leaving it up to you to decide what features you want to add.

With Flask, you can create dynamic web pages, handle user input, and interact with databases. Unlike some other web frameworks, Flask doesn't force you to follow a strict structure, which gives you the flexibility to organize your project as you see fit.

Typical Python Web Application Request Flow

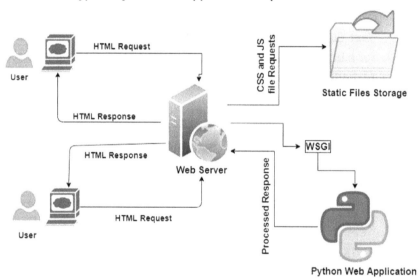

In this chapter, we will walk through the following key topics:

- **Setting up Flask**

- **Building a simple web application**

- **Working with routes, templates, and forms**

---

1. Setting Up Flask

Setting up Flask is simple and quick. Let's get started by creating a basic Flask application.

Creating Your First Flask App

1. Open your text editor and create a new file called app.py (you can name it anything, but app.py is the convention).

2. Import Flask and create an instance of it.

Example:

```python

from flask import Flask

# Create an instance of the Flask class
app = Flask(__name__)

# Define a route for the homepage
@app.route('/')
def home():
    return "Hello, Flask!"

# Run the app
```

```
if __name__ == '__main__':
    app.run(debug=True)
```

Explanation:

- **Flask(__name__):** This creates a Flask application. The __name__ variable helps Flask determine where to look for templates and static files.

- **@app.route('/'):** This is a **route decorator** that tells Flask what URL should trigger the home() function. The / route corresponds to the homepage.

- **app.run(debug=True):** This runs the app and enables **debug mode**, which allows you to see error messages in the browser if something goes wrong.

Running Your Flask App

1. Save the file as app.py.

2. Open your terminal and navigate to the folder where app.py is saved.

3. Run the application by typing:

bash

```
python app.py
```

You should see something like this in the terminal:

bash

```
* Running on http://127.0.0.1:5000/ (Press CTRL+C to quit)
```

Now open your web browser and go to http://127.0.0.1:5000/. You should see the message **"Hello, Flask!"**.

2. Building a Simple Web Application

Now that you have Flask set up, let's build a simple web application. We'll create a small **blog** where users can view blog posts and submit new ones.

Step 1: Creating Routes for the Blog

We'll start by defining routes for the homepage and a page to submit new blog posts.

```python
from flask import Flask, render_template, request

app = Flask(__name__)

# A simple list to hold blog posts (in memory)
posts = [
    {"title": "My First Blog Post", "content": "Welcome to my blog!"},
    {"title": "Another Blog Post", "content": "Here's another post."},
]

@app.route('/')
def home():
    return render_template('home.html', posts=posts)

@app.route('/new', methods=['GET', 'POST'])
def new_post():
    if request.method == 'POST':
        title = request.form['title']
```

```
        content = request.form['content']
        posts.append({"title": title, "content": content})
        return redirect('/')
    return render_template('new_post.html')


if __name__ == '__main__':
    app.run(debug=True)
```

Explanation:

- **home()**: This route renders the homepage and displays a list of blog posts.

- **new_post()**: This route handles both GET and POST requests. It displays a form to submit new blog posts (using new_post.html) and adds the post to the list when submitted.

- **request.form**: This is used to get data from the form submitted by the user.

Step 2: Creating HTML Templates

Flask uses templates to render dynamic HTML. Templates allow us to use Python-like syntax inside HTML files.

1. Create a new folder named **templates** in the same directory as app.py.

2. Inside the **templates** folder, create two HTML files:

   - **home.html**

   - **new_post.html**

home.html (for the homepage):

```
html
```

```html
<!DOCTYPE html>
<html lang="en">
<head>
    <meta charset="UTF-8">
    <meta name="viewport" content="width=device-width, initial-scale=1.0">
    <title>My Blog</title>
</head>
<body>
    <h1>Welcome to My Blog</h1>
    <ul>
        {% for post in posts %}
            <li>
                <h2>{{ post.title }}</h2>
                <p>{{ post.content }}</p>
            </li>
        {% endfor %}
    </ul>
    <a href="/new">Create New Post</a>
</body>
</html>
```

new_post.html (for submitting a new post):

html

```html
<!DOCTYPE html>
<html lang="en">
<head>
    <meta charset="UTF-8">
```

```html
<meta name="viewport" content="width=device-width, initial-scale=1.0">
<title>New Blog Post</title>
</head>
<body>
  <h1>Create a New Blog Post</h1>
  <form action="/new" method="POST">
    <label for="title">Title:</label>
    <input type="text" id="title" name="title" required><br>

    <label for="content">Content:</label>
    <textarea id="content" name="content" required></textarea><br>

    <button type="submit">Submit</button>
  </form>
</body>
</html>
```

Explanation:

- **home.html**: Displays a list of blog posts dynamically using Jinja syntax ({% for post in posts %} and {{ post.title }}).

- **new_post.html**: A form that allows users to submit a new blog post. The form sends a POST request with the title and content to the /new route.

Step 3: Running the Blog Application

Now, run app.py again:

bash

```bash
python app.py
```

In your browser, go to **http://127.0.0.1:5000/** to view the blog's homepage. You can click **Create New Post** to add a new post.

---

3. Working with Routes, Templates, and Forms

Let's explore **routes**, **templates**, and **forms** in more detail, as they are key concepts in Flask development.

Understanding Routes

A **route** in Flask is a URL pattern that is linked to a function. The function associated with a route is executed whenever a request is made to that route. Routes are defined using the @app.route decorator.

Example:

```python
@app.route('/')
def home():
    return "Welcome to the homepage!"
```

Explanation:

- The route '/' is the URL for the homepage. When a user navigates to this URL, the home() function is called and its return value is displayed.

Templates in Flask

Templates are HTML files with embedded Python-like expressions. Flask uses **Jinja2** for templating, which allows you to include Python code in the form of placeholders and logic.

Example:

```html
html
```

```html
<h1>Welcome, {{ username }}!</h1>
```

Explanation:

- {{ username }} is a placeholder that Flask will replace with the actual value of username when rendering the template.

Handling Forms in Flask

Forms are an essential part of web applications. In Flask, you can handle form data using request.form when the form is submitted via a POST request.

Example:

```python
python
```

```python
from flask import request

@app.route('/submit', methods=['POST'])
def submit_form():
    username = request.form['username']
    email = request.form['email']
    return f"Submitted: {username}, {email}"
```

Explanation:

- request.form['username'] and request.form['email'] retrieve the values submitted in the form.

Key Takeaways

- **Flask Setup**: Flask is lightweight and easy to get started with. It allows you to define routes and render dynamic HTML templates.

- **Routes**: Routes define the paths in your application and map them to Python functions that return data or HTML.

- **Templates**: Jinja2 templates help render dynamic HTML by injecting Python variables and expressions into the HTML structure.

- **Forms**: Forms allow you to gather user input and send it to the server. You can then process the input in your routes.

Chapter 7: Data Science Basics – Pandas and NumPy

What You'll Need

Before we begin, let's make sure you have the right tools in place:

1. **A Computer**: This chapter will work on Windows, macOS, and Linux.

2. **Python Installed**: Ensure you have Python 3.x installed. You can download the latest version from python.org.

3. **Python Libraries**: You will need the following libraries:

   o **Pandas**: For data manipulation and analysis.

   o **NumPy**: For numerical computing and working with arrays.

To install these libraries, open your terminal or command prompt and type the following:

bash

pip install pandas numpy

Once installed, you're all set to dive into data science!

Introduction to Data Science

Data Science is the field that uses various methods, processes, and systems to extract knowledge and insights from data. It is a rapidly growing field that combines **statistics**, **computer science**, and **domain knowledge** to make sense of vast amounts of data.

Data science helps answer important questions, such as:

- How can we predict future sales for a business?

- What are the factors that influence a customer's decision to buy a product?

- How can we identify anomalies or fraud in financial transactions?

Python is one of the most popular programming languages for data science because of its simplicity and the availability of powerful libraries like **Pandas** and **NumPy**, which are essential tools in the data science toolbox.

In this chapter, we'll explore two of these libraries—Pandas and NumPy—and see how they can help you manipulate and analyze data.

---

1. Data Manipulation with Pandas

Pandas is a Python library that provides powerful, easy-to-use data structures for data manipulation and analysis. It is especially useful for working with **tabular data**, such as datasets represented as **tables** (think of an Excel spreadsheet or SQL database).

1.1 Introduction to Pandas Data Structures

Pandas has two main data structures:

- **Series**: A one-dimensional array-like object.

- **DataFrame**: A two-dimensional table, similar to a spreadsheet, where data is stored in rows and columns.

Creating a Pandas Series

A **Series** is like a list or an array, but it has additional functionality like labeled axes (rows). You can create a Series from a Python list or a dictionary.

Example 1: Creating a Series

```python
import pandas as pd

# Creating a Series from a list
data = [10, 20, 30, 40, 50]
series = pd.Series(data)
print(series)
```

Explanation:

- pd.Series(data) creates a Series object from the list data.

- Pandas automatically assigns indices to each item (0, 1, 2, etc.).

Creating a DataFrame

A **DataFrame** is a two-dimensional table that can store data in rows and columns. Each column can have a different data type (e.g., strings, integers, floats).

Example 2: Creating a DataFrame

```python
data = {
    'Name': ['Alice', 'Bob', 'Charlie', 'David', 'Eve'],
    'Age': [25, 30, 35, 40, 45],
    'Salary': [50000, 60000, 70000, 80000, 90000]
}

df = pd.DataFrame(data)
print(df)
```

Explanation:

- The pd.DataFrame(data) creates a DataFrame from a dictionary where the keys are column names, and the values are lists that represent the data for each column.

- The resulting DataFrame is displayed in a tabular format.

1.2 Working with DataFrames

Once you have a DataFrame, you can easily manipulate and analyze data.

Accessing Columns and Rows

You can access columns in a DataFrame using the column name (as an attribute or with square brackets) and rows using **loc** (label-based) or **iloc** (position-based).

Example 3: Accessing Columns

```python
# Accessing a column by name
print(df['Name'])  # Output: Series of names

# Accessing a column using attribute-style access
print(df.Name)  # Output: Series of names
```

Example 4: Accessing Rows by Index

```python
# Accessing a row by index (position-based)
print(df.iloc[1])  # Output: Row at index 1 (Bob's details)

# Accessing a row by label (name-based)
print(df.loc[2])  # Output: Row for Charlie
```

Example 5: Filtering Data

You can filter data based on conditions. For example, let's filter the DataFrame to find employees older than 30.

```python
older_than_30 = df[df['Age'] > 30]
print(older_than_30)
```

Explanation:

- df['Age'] > 30 creates a boolean mask (True/False values) that is used to filter the DataFrame.

1.3 Modifying Data

You can modify the content of a DataFrame by adding new columns, changing values, or dropping rows/columns.

Example 6: Adding a New Column

```python
df['Bonus'] = [5000, 6000, 7000, 8000, 9000]
print(df)
```

Explanation:

- A new column, Bonus, is added to the DataFrame with values for each employee.

Example 7: Modifying Values

```python
df.loc[0, 'Salary'] = 55000  # Modify the salary of the first row (Alice)
print(df)
```

Explanation:

- df.loc[0, 'Salary'] modifies the value of the Salary column for the row with index 0.

Example 8: Dropping Rows or Columns

```python
df = df.drop(columns=['Bonus'])  # Drop the 'Bonus' column
df = df.drop(2)  # Drop the row at index 2 (Charlie's details)
print(df)
```

Explanation:

- df.drop(columns=['Bonus']) removes the 'Bonus' column.

- df.drop(2) removes the row with index 2.

---

2. Using NumPy for Numerical Computing

NumPy is another essential library in Python, primarily used for numerical and scientific computing. NumPy provides support for arrays (n-dimensional), matrices, and mathematical functions to perform operations on these arrays.

2.1 Introduction to NumPy Arrays

A **NumPy array** is similar to a Python list but more efficient for numerical operations. NumPy arrays are **homogeneous** (they can only hold items of the same type), which makes them faster and more memory-efficient than Python lists.

Example 1: Creating NumPy Arrays

```python
import numpy as np

# Creating a 1D NumPy array
arr = np.array([1, 2, 3, 4, 5])
print(arr)

# Creating a 2D NumPy array
arr_2d = np.array([[1, 2], [3, 4], [5, 6]])
print(arr_2d)
```

Explanation:

- np.array() creates a NumPy array. You can create both 1D and 2D arrays.

2.2 Basic Operations with NumPy

NumPy arrays allow you to perform mathematical operations easily and efficiently.

Example 2: Element-wise Operations

```python
python

arr = np.array([1, 2, 3, 4, 5])

# Adding 10 to each element
arr_plus_10 = arr + 10
print(arr_plus_10)  # Output: [11 12 13 14 15]

# Multiplying each element by 2
arr_times_2 = arr * 2
print(arr_times_2)  # Output: [2 4 6 8 10]
```

Explanation:

- NumPy allows you to add, subtract, multiply, and divide arrays element-wise.

Example 3: Matrix Multiplication

NumPy makes it easy to perform matrix operations.

```
python

arr1 = np.array([[1, 2], [3, 4]])
arr2 = np.array([[5, 6], [7, 8]])

# Matrix multiplication
result = np.dot(arr1, arr2)
print(result)
```

Explanation:

- np.dot() performs matrix multiplication, which is different from element-wise multiplication.

2.3 Advanced NumPy Functions

NumPy provides a wide range of mathematical functions that can be applied to arrays, such as computing the sum, mean, and standard deviation.

Example 4: Aggregate Functions

```
python

arr = np.array([1, 2, 3, 4, 5])

# Sum of elements
print(np.sum(arr)) # Output: 15

# Mean of elements
print(np.mean(arr)) # Output: 3.0

# Standard deviation of elements
print(np.std(arr)) # Output: 1.4142135623730951
```

Explanation:

- np.sum(), np.mean(), and np.std() are used to calculate the sum, mean, and standard deviation of array elements, respectively.

---

3. Practical Project: Analyzing Sales Data

Let's apply what we've learned with a simple project. Suppose you are working for a company that wants to analyze sales data to calculate some basic statistics and trends.

Step 1: Loading and Exploring the Data

First, we need a dataset. Let's simulate a simple sales dataset using Pandas.

```python
import pandas as pd

# Creating a sample sales dataset
data = {
    'Product': ['A', 'B', 'C', 'D', 'E'],
    'Units Sold': [100, 200, 150, 300, 250],
    'Price Per Unit': [10, 15, 12, 20, 18]
}

df = pd.DataFrame(data)
print(df)
```

Explanation:

- We created a dataset of products with the number of units sold and the price per unit.

Step 2: Adding a Total Sales Column

Now let's calculate the total sales for each product.

python

```python
df['Total Sales'] = df['Units Sold'] * df['Price Per Unit']
print(df)
```

Explanation:

- We multiply the Units Sold by the Price Per Unit to calculate the Total Sales.

Step 3: Using NumPy for Advanced Calculations

We can also use NumPy to calculate more advanced statistics, such as the total sales mean and standard deviation.

python

```python
import numpy as np

# Calculate the mean and standard deviation of total sales
mean_sales = np.mean(df['Total Sales'])
std_sales = np.std(df['Total Sales'])

print(f"Mean Sales: {mean_sales}")
print(f"Standard Deviation of Sales: {std_sales}")
```

Explanation:

- We use np.mean() and np.std() to calculate the mean and standard deviation of total sales.

- **Pandas** is an essential tool for data manipulation and analysis, allowing you to easily handle and transform datasets.

- **NumPy** is powerful for numerical computing, enabling you to perform efficient calculations on large datasets.

- By combining **Pandas** and **NumPy**, you can handle and analyze real-world datasets in Python with ease.

Chapter 8: Data Visualization with Matplotlib

What You'll Need

Before we dive into the world of data visualization, let's make sure you have everything set up:

1. **A Computer**: This chapter will work on Windows, macOS, and Linux systems.

2. **Python Installed**: You need Python 3.x installed. You can download the latest version from python.org.

3. **Libraries**:

   o **Matplotlib**: The primary library for data visualization.

   o **Pandas**: For handling and manipulating data before plotting.

   o **NumPy**: For numerical operations, especially when working with large datasets.

To install these libraries, run the following commands in your terminal/command prompt:

bash

pip install matplotlib pandas numpy

Once you have all the necessary libraries installed, you're ready to start creating powerful visualizations!

Understanding Data Visualization

Data visualization is the graphical representation of data and information. By using visual elements like charts, graphs, and maps, data visualization tools provide an accessible way to see and understand trends, outliers, and patterns in data.

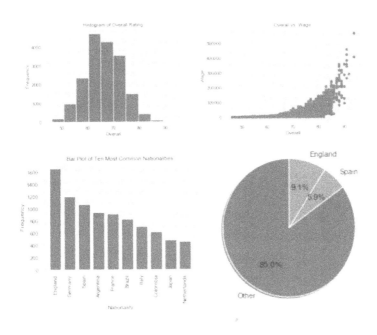

Data visualization is crucial in many fields, including:

- **Business Intelligence**: To make informed decisions based on sales data, customer behavior, etc.

- **Healthcare**: To analyze and communicate health statistics.

- **Finance**: To visualize market trends, stock prices, and other financial data.

- **Manufacturing**: To analyze production efficiency and supply chain metrics.

Visualizing data helps make sense of large datasets and enables easier interpretation. Matplotlib, one of the most popular Python libraries for data visualization, is a powerful tool for creating static, animated, and interactive visualizations in Python.

---

1. Plotting Graphs and Charts with Matplotlib

Matplotlib is the go-to library for creating static plots. It allows you to create a wide range of graphs, from simple line charts to complex scatter plots and heatmaps. Let's start with the basics.

Creating Your First Plot: Line Graph

Line graphs are useful for visualizing trends over time or other continuous variables. To create a line graph in Matplotlib, you use the plot() function.

Example 1: Basic Line Plot

```python
python

import matplotlib.pyplot as plt

# Data for plotting
x = [0, 1, 2, 3, 4]
y = [0, 1, 4, 9, 16]

# Create a simple line plot
plt.plot(x, y)
```

```python
# Display the plot
plt.show()
```

Explanation:

x and y are the data points for the graph.

plt.plot(x, y) creates the line plot, with x as the horizontal axis and y as the vertical axis.

plt.show() displays the plot in a window.

Customizing Line Graphs

Matplotlib allows you to customize your plot in various ways, such as adding labels, changing line colors, and adjusting axis limits.

Example 2: Customizing Line Plot

```python
python

import matplotlib.pyplot as plt

# Data for plotting
x = [0, 1, 2, 3, 4]
y = [0, 1, 4, 9, 16]

# Create a line plot with customization
plt.plot(x, y, color='blue', linewidth=2, marker='o', markersize=8)

# Add title and labels
plt.title('Basic Line Plot')
plt.xlabel('X Values')
plt.ylabel('Y Values')
```

```
# Display the plot
plt.show()
```

Explanation:

- color='blue' changes the line color to blue.

- linewidth=2 adjusts the thickness of the line.

- marker='o' adds circular markers at each data point, and markersize=8 increases their size.

- plt.title(), plt.xlabel(), and plt.ylabel() add the title and axis labels.

---

2. Working with Bar Charts

Bar charts are used to compare quantities across different categories. In Matplotlib, you can create bar charts using the bar() function.

Example 3: Simple Bar Chart

```python
import matplotlib.pyplot as plt

# Data for plotting
categories = ['A', 'B', 'C', 'D', 'E']
values = [3, 7, 2, 5, 6]

# Create a bar chart
plt.bar(categories, values)
```

```python
# Add title and labels
plt.title('Simple Bar Chart')
plt.xlabel('Categories')
plt.ylabel('Values')

# Display the plot
plt.show()
```

Explanation:

- plt.bar(categories, values) creates a bar chart with the specified categories and values.

- Just like with the line plot, you can add a title and axis labels.

Example 4: Horizontal Bar Chart

You can also create horizontal bar charts using the barh() function.

```python
python

import matplotlib.pyplot as plt

# Data for plotting
categories = ['A', 'B', 'C', 'D', 'E']
values = [3, 7, 2, 5, 6]

# Create a horizontal bar chart
plt.barh(categories, values)

# Add title and labels
plt.title('Horizontal Bar Chart')
plt.xlabel('Values')
```

```
plt.ylabel('Categories')

# Display the plot
plt.show()
```

Explanation:

- plt.barh() switches the bars to be horizontal.

---

3. Creating Histograms

A histogram is a graph that shows the distribution of a dataset. It groups data into bins and displays how many data points fall into each bin.

Example 5: Simple Histogram

```python
import matplotlib.pyplot as plt
import numpy as np

# Data for plotting (randomly generated data)
data = np.random.randn(1000)

# Create a histogram
plt.hist(data, bins=30, edgecolor='black')

# Add title and labels
plt.title('Histogram of Random Data')
plt.xlabel('Value')
plt.ylabel('Frequency')
```

```
# Display the plot
plt.show()
```

Explanation:

- np.random.randn(1000) generates 1000 random numbers from a normal distribution.

- plt.hist() creates a histogram with 30 bins. The edgecolor='black' option adds black borders to the bins for clarity.

---

4. Customizing Plots

One of the strengths of Matplotlib is its ability to customize every aspect of the plot. Let's explore a few ways to tweak your visualizations.

Example 6: Adding Legends

Legends are useful when you have multiple lines or plots on the same graph, as they help differentiate between them.

```python
import matplotlib.pyplot as plt

# Data for plotting
x = [0, 1, 2, 3, 4]
y1 = [0, 1, 4, 9, 16]
y2 = [0, 2, 4, 6, 8]

# Create two line plots
```

```python
plt.plot(x, y1, label='y = x^2', color='blue')
plt.plot(x, y2, label='y = 2x', color='red')

# Add title, labels, and legend
plt.title('Multiple Line Plots')
plt.xlabel('X Values')
plt.ylabel('Y Values')
plt.legend()

# Display the plot
plt.show()
```

Explanation:

- label='y = x^2' and label='y = 2x' are used to define the labels for the lines.

- plt.legend() displays the legend in the plot.

Example 7: Customizing Plot Style

You can customize the plot style using predefined styles in Matplotlib.

```python
python

import matplotlib.pyplot as plt

# Use a predefined style
plt.style.use('seaborn-darkgrid')

# Data for plotting
x = [0, 1, 2, 3, 4]
```

```python
y = [0, 1, 4, 9, 16]

# Create a simple plot with a custom style
plt.plot(x, y)

# Add title and labels
plt.title('Styled Line Plot')
plt.xlabel('X Values')
plt.ylabel('Y Values')

# Display the plot
plt.show()
```

Explanation:

- plt.style.use('seaborn-darkgrid') applies the seaborn-darkgrid style, which provides a grid background and enhanced visuals for the plot.

---

5. Scatter Plots

A **scatter plot** is useful for showing the relationship between two continuous variables. Each point represents a data point with two variables: one on the x-axis and one on the y-axis.

Example 8: Simple Scatter Plot

```python
python
```

```python
import matplotlib.pyplot as plt

# Data for plotting
x = [1, 2, 3, 4, 5]
y = [5, 4, 3, 2, 1]

# Create a scatter plot
plt.scatter(x, y)

# Add title and labels
plt.title('Simple Scatter Plot')
plt.xlabel('X Values')
plt.ylabel('Y Values')

# Display the plot
plt.show()
```

Explanation:

- plt.scatter() creates a scatter plot by plotting points at the (x, y) coordinates.

---

6. Working with Multiple Subplots

Sometimes, you may want to display multiple plots in one figure. Matplotlib allows you to create subplots (multiple graphs in a single window) using plt.subplot().

Example 9: Multiple Subplots

python

```python
import matplotlib.pyplot as plt
import numpy as np

# Create two subplots
fig, (ax1, ax2) = plt.subplots(1, 2)

# Data for plotting
x = np.linspace(0, 10, 100)
y1 = np.sin(x)
y2 = np.cos(x)

# Plot on the first subplot
ax1.plot(x, y1, color='blue')
ax1.set_title('Sine Wave')

# Plot on the second subplot
ax2.plot(x, y2, color='red')
ax2.set_title('Cosine Wave')

# Display the plot
plt.show()
```

Explanation:

- plt.subplots(1, 2) creates a figure with 1 row and 2 columns of subplots.

- ax1 and ax2 represent the individual axes (subplots) in the figure.

- **Matplotlib** is a powerful library for creating a wide range of static, animated, and interactive plots in Python.

- You can create various types of plots, such as line charts, bar charts, histograms, and scatter plots, to visualize data.

- Customizing your plots is easy with options to change colors, labels, styles, and much more.

- **Subplots** allow you to display multiple visualizations in a single window, which is useful for comparing different datasets or trends.

Chapter 9: Automation with Python: Scripts for Everyday Tasks

Before we dive into automation, let's make sure you have everything set up:

1. **A Computer**: Python can be used on any operating system: Windows, macOS, or Linux.

2. **Python Installed**: Ensure that Python 3.x is installed on your machine. You can download the latest version from python.org.

3. **Python Libraries**: To automate tasks, you'll need some specific libraries:

    o   **os**: For interacting with the operating system.

    o   **shutil**: For file operations like ing, moving, and deleting.

    o   **requests**: For making HTTP requests, often used for web scraping.

    o   **BeautifulSoup**: For parsing HTML and XML content in web scraping.

You can install the libraries **requests** and **beautifulsoup4** by running:

```
bash
```

```
pip install requests beautifulsoup4
```

Once you have everything in place, you're ready to start automating!

Introduction to Automation

Automation is the process of using technology to perform tasks without human intervention. In the context of programming, automation refers to writing scripts to automate repetitive tasks on your computer or across the web. Python is an excellent tool for automation because it is simple, powerful, and has a vast collection of libraries to support various tasks.

Automation can make your life much easier, whether you're managing files on your computer, gathering information from websites, or even sending emails and managing schedules.

In this chapter, we'll cover:

1. **Automating File Management**
2. **Writing Web Scraping Scripts**

---

1. Automating File Management

Managing files on your computer can be time-consuming, especially if you frequently have to move, rename, or organize them. With Python, you can automate these tasks to save time and avoid mistakes. The **os** and **shutil** libraries provide functions that allow you to interact with the operating system, such as creating folders, renaming files, or ing files.

1.1 Creating Directories and Files

First, let's look at how you can automate creating directories and files.

Example 1: Create a Directory and File

Let's create a directory and a text file within it.

```python
import os

# Define the directory and file name
directory = "new_folder"
file_name = "example.txt"

# Create a directory
if not os.path.exists(directory):
    os.makedirs(directory)
    print(f"Directory '{directory}' created.")

# Create a file inside the directory
file_path = os.path.join(directory, file_name)
with open(file_path, 'w') as file:
    file.write("This is an automated file.")
    print(f"File '{file_name}' created inside '{directory}'.")
```

Explanation:

- os.makedirs() creates a new directory if it doesn't exist already.

- os.path.join() combines the directory path and file name to create the full file path.

- open() is used to create and write to the file. In this case, we're writing a string to the file.

1.2 Renaming Files

Renaming files can be tedious if you have many files to process. Python makes it easy to automate this with os.rename().

Example 2: Rename Files in a Directory

Let's say you have a folder with files that need to be renamed. Here's how you can do it programmatically.

```python
import os

# Directory containing files
directory = "my_folder"

# Iterate over the files in the directory
for filename in os.listdir(directory):
    old_path = os.path.join(directory, filename)

    # Check if the item is a file
    if os.path.isfile(old_path):
        new_name = "new_" + filename
        new_path = os.path.join(directory, new_name)
```

```
os.rename(old_path, new_path)
print(f"Renamed '{filename}' to '{new_name}'")
```

Explanation:

- os.listdir(directory) lists all files and directories in the given folder.

- os.path.isfile() ensures that we only rename files (not directories).

- os.rename() is used to rename the files by appending new_ to the original file name.

1.3 Moving and ing Files

You may also want to move or files to different locations. The shutil module makes this easy.

Example 3: Move Files to a New Folder

Here's how to move files from one folder to another.

```python
import shutil
import os

# Define source and destination paths
source = "source_folder/my_file.txt"
destination = "destination_folder/my_file.txt"

# Move the file
shutil.move(source, destination)
print(f"Moved file from {source} to {destination}")
```

Explanation:

- shutil.move() moves the file from the source path to the destination path. If the destination folder doesn't exist, it will be created.

Example 4: Files

If you want to files instead of moving them, use shutil.().

```python
import shutil

# Define source and destination paths
source = "source_folder/my_file.txt"
destination = "destination_folder/my_file.txt"

# the file
shutil.(source, destination)
print(f"Copied file from {source} to {destination}")
```

Explanation:

- shutil.() copies the file to the destination without deleting the original.

---

2. Writing Web Scraping Scripts

Web scraping is the process of extracting data from websites. This can be useful for gathering data from news articles, product prices, or any publicly available web information.

We will use two Python libraries for web scraping:

1. **requests**: To send HTTP requests to a website.

2. **BeautifulSoup**: To parse and extract data from HTML content.

2.1 Sending HTTP Requests

To retrieve the content of a webpage, we first need to send an HTTP request to the website's URL. The requests library helps with this.

Example 1: Fetching a Web Page

```python
import requests

# Define the URL of the website
url = "https://example.com"

# Send an HTTP GET request to the URL
response = requests.get(url)

# Print the response content (HTML)
print(response.text)
```

Explanation:

- requests.get(url) sends a GET request to the URL and stores the response in the response object.

- response.text contains the raw HTML content of the page.

2.2 Parsing HTML with BeautifulSoup

Once we have the HTML content of a webpage, we need to parse it to extract specific information. This is where **BeautifulSoup** comes in.

Example 2: Extracting Titles from a Web Page

Let's extract the titles of articles from a website.

```python
import requests
from bs4 import BeautifulSoup

# Define the URL of the website
url = "https://example.com"

# Send an HTTP GET request
response = requests.get(url)

# Parse the HTML content
soup = BeautifulSoup(response.text, 'html.parser')

# Find all article titles (assuming they are inside <h2> tags)
titles = soup.find_all('h2')

# Print each title
for title in titles:
    print(title.get_text())
```

Explanation:

- BeautifulSoup(response.text, 'html.parser') parses the HTML content of the page.

- soup.find_all('h2') finds all <h2> tags on the page, which we assume contain article titles.

- title.get_text() extracts the text from each title tag.

2.3 Handling Web Scraping Challenges

Web scraping can be challenging due to dynamic content (content loaded via JavaScript), anti-scraping measures, and site structure variations. In these cases, you might need to use tools like **Selenium** for dynamic scraping or work with APIs if the website provides one.

Example 3: Scraping Dynamic Content (using Selenium)

Selenium can be used to interact with JavaScript-loaded web pages.

```python
from selenium import webdriver

# Open a browser window
driver = webdriver.Chrome()

# Navigate to the page
driver.get("https://example.com")

# Wait for content to load (implicitly wait for 5 seconds)
driver.implicitly_wait(5)

# Extract the page source
html = driver.page_source

# Parse the HTML
soup = BeautifulSoup(html, 'html.parser')

# Find and print the titles
titles = soup.find_all('h2')
```

```
for title in titles:
    print(title.get_text())

# Close the browser window
driver.quit()
```

Explanation:

- Selenium opens a browser and interacts with the page just like a human would.

- driver.page_source retrieves the HTML after the page has fully loaded.

Practical Projects: Automating Daily Tasks

Let's combine what we've learned into a few practical projects that automate everyday tasks.

Project 1: File Organization Script

Imagine you have a folder filled with files that need to be sorted into subfolders based on their file extension (e.g., .txt, .pdf, .jpg). Here's how to automate this task.

```python

import os
import shutil

# Define the source directory
source_dir = "downloads"
```

```
# Create subfolders for each file type
for filename in os.listdir(source_dir):
    file_path = os.path.join(source_dir, filename)

    if os.path.isfile(file_path):
        file_extension = filename.split('.')[-1]
        target_dir = os.path.join(source_dir, file_extension)

        # Create the subfolder if it doesn't exist
        if not os.path.exists(target_dir):
            os.makedirs(target_dir)

        # Move the file to the corresponding subfolder
        shutil.move(file_path, os.path.join(target_dir, filename))
        print(f"Moved {filename} to {target_dir}")
```

Explanation:

- The script iterates over all files in the downloads directory, extracts the file extension, and moves each file to its corresponding subfolder (e.g., .txt files to a "txt" folder).

Project 2: Web Scraping Script for Job Listings

You can automate the process of checking job listings from websites. Let's scrape job titles from a hypothetical job listing site.

```python
import requests
from bs4 import BeautifulSoup
```

```python
# Define the URL of the job listing site
url = "https://jobsite.com/jobs"

# Send an HTTP request
response = requests.get(url)

# Parse the HTML
soup = BeautifulSoup(response.text, 'html.parser')

# Find and print job titles
job_titles = soup.find_all('h3', class_='job-title')
for job in job_titles:
    print(job.get_text())
```

Explanation:

- The script fetches the HTML of the job listings page and extracts the job titles by finding all <h3> tags with a specific class.

Key Takeaways

- **Automation with Python** can make repetitive tasks much easier and more efficient.

- **File management**: You can automate file organization, renaming, moving, and ing using the os and shutil libraries.

- **Web scraping**: Python's requests and BeautifulSoup allow you to extract data from web pages, saving time and effort in manual data collection.

- **Real-World Application**: These automation skills can be applied to a wide range of industries, such as data collection, file management, and web scraping for analysis.

Chapter 10: Interacting with APIs: Fetching Data from the Web

What You'll Need

Before you start interacting with APIs, let's make sure you have everything set up:

1. **A Computer**: Python can run on all operating systems, including Windows, macOS, and Linux.

2. **Python Installed**: Ensure Python 3.x is installed. You can download it from python.org.

3. **Libraries**:

   o   **requests**: For making HTTP requests to web APIs.

   o   **json**: For parsing JSON data from API responses.

To install the **requests** library, open your terminal/command prompt and run:

bash

pip install requests

Once you have everything set up, you're ready to start working with APIs!

Introduction to APIs and HTTP Requests

API stands for **Application Programming Interface**. An API allows different software systems to communicate with each other. When you use an API, you're asking one application to retrieve information or perform tasks that you can then use in your own application.

In the context of web APIs, we often send **HTTP requests** to a web server, which processes the request and returns data (usually in **JSON** or **XML** format).

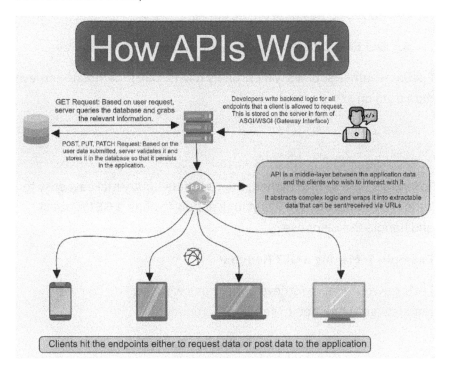

What is HTTP?

HTTP (HyperText Transfer Protocol) is the protocol used to request and send data on the web. When you interact with a website (by entering a URL in the browser), your browser sends an HTTP request to that server. The server then sends back an HTTP response.

Types of HTTP Requests

When interacting with APIs, we typically use the following types of HTTP requests:

1. **GET**: Retrieves data from the server (e.g., fetching weather data, news, etc.).

2. **POST**: Sends data to the server (e.g., submitting a form, posting data).

3. **PUT**: Updates data on the server.

4. **DELETE**: Deletes data from the server.

For our weather app, we will primarily use the **GET** method to retrieve data from an API.

---

1. Making HTTP Requests with Python

To interact with APIs in Python, the **requests** library makes it easy to send HTTP requests. We'll first look at how to send a **GET** request and handle the response.

Example 1: Making a GET Request

Let's say you want to retrieve data from a website. You can use the requests.get() function to send a GET request.

```python
import requests

# Define the URL of the API (example placeholder)
url = "https://jsonplaceholder.typicode.com/posts"
```

```python
# Send a GET request
response = requests.get(url)

# Print the response text (raw HTML or JSON)
print(response.text)
```

Explanation:

- requests.get(url) sends a GET request to the URL and returns the response.

- response.text contains the raw content of the response (in this case, the JSON data from the API).

Handling API Responses

When you send a request, the server will respond with a status code, along with the data you requested. It's important to check the status code to ensure the request was successful.

Example 2: Checking the Response Status

```python
python

import requests

url = "https://jsonplaceholder.typicode.com/posts"
response = requests.get(url)

# Check if the request was successful
if response.status_code == 200:
    print("Request was successful!")
    print(response.json())  # Parse the JSON data
```

```
else:
    print(f"Request failed with status code {response.status_code}")
```

Explanation:

- response.status_code gives the HTTP status code returned by the server (200 means success).

- response.json() parses the response content as JSON and returns it as a Python dictionary.

---

2. Working with JSON Data

When working with APIs, the data returned is usually in **JSON** format. JSON (JavaScript Object Notation) is a lightweight data format used to exchange data between a server and a client. Python's json module makes it easy to work with JSON data.

Understanding JSON

A typical JSON response looks like this:

```json
{
    "id": 1,
    "title": "My first post",
    "body": "This is the content of my first post."
}
```

JSON data consists of key-value pairs, where:

- **Keys** are strings (e.g., "id", "title", "body").

- **Values** can be various data types like strings, numbers, arrays, or other JSON objects.

Example 3: Parsing JSON Data

Let's retrieve a list of posts from a JSON API and display them.

```python
import requests

# Send a GET request to retrieve data
url = "https://jsonplaceholder.typicode.com/posts"
response = requests.get(url)

# Check if the request was successful
if response.status_code == 200:
    # Parse the JSON data
    posts = response.json()

    # Print each post's title and body
    for post in posts:
        print(f"Title: {post['title']}")
        print(f"Body: {post['body']}\n")
else:
    print(f"Request failed with status code {response.status_code}")
```

Explanation:

- The response.json() method converts the JSON response into a Python list of dictionaries.

- We loop over the list of posts and print out the title and body for each post.

3. Building a Weather App Using an API

Now that we've covered the basics of making requests and handling JSON data, let's build a simple weather app using an API. We will fetch weather data from a free API called **OpenWeatherMap**.

Step 1: Setting Up the OpenWeatherMap API

1. Go to the OpenWeatherMap API website and sign up for a free API key.

2. After signing up, you'll be given an **API key**. This key is used to authenticate your requests.

Step 2: Fetching Weather Data

Let's use the API to get the current weather for a city. For this example, we will fetch the weather for **London**.

```python
import requests

# Define your API key and the URL for the OpenWeatherMap API
api_key = "your_api_key_here"
city = "London"
url = f"http://api.openweathermap.org/data/2.5/weather?q={city}&appid={api_key}&units=metric"

# Send a GET request to fetch weather data
response = requests.get(url)
```

```python
# Check if the request was successful
if response.status_code == 200:
    # Parse the JSON data
    data = response.json()

    # Extract the weather details
    temperature = data['main']['temp']
    weather_description = data['weather'][0]['description']
    city_name = data['name']

    # Display the weather information
    print(f"Weather in {city_name}:")
    print(f"Temperature: {temperature}°C")
    print(f"Condition: {weather_description.capitalize()}")
else:
    print(f"Failed to retrieve data. Status code: {response.status_code}")
```

Explanation:

- The URL includes the API key, city name, and a request for **metric units** (Celsius).

- The response.json() method parses the returned JSON data into a Python dictionary.

- We extract the temperature and weather condition from the JSON data and display it.

Step 3: Making the App Interactive

Let's make the app more interactive by asking the user for a city name and showing the weather for that city.

```python
import requests

# Define the function to get weather data
def get_weather(city):
    api_key = "your_api_key_here"
    url = f"http://api.openweathermap.org/data/2.5/weather?q={city}&appid={api_key}&units=metric"

    # Send the GET request
    response = requests.get(url)

    # Check if the request was successful
    if response.status_code == 200:
        data = response.json()
        temperature = data['main']['temp']
        weather_description = data['weather'][0]['description']
        city_name = data['name']

        # Return the weather data
        return city_name, temperature, weather_description
    else:
        return None, None, None

# Ask the user for a city name
city = input("Enter the name of a city: ")
```

116

```python
# Get the weather data
city_name, temperature, weather_description = get_weather(city)

if city_name:
    print(f"Weather in {city_name}:")
    print(f"Temperature: {temperature}°C")
    print(f"Condition: {weather_description.capitalize()}")
else:
    print("City not found or there was an error retrieving the data.")
```

Explanation:

- The get_weather() function takes the city name, sends a request to the OpenWeatherMap API, and returns the city name, temperature, and weather description.

- The input() function allows the user to enter a city name dynamically.

Key Takeaways

- **APIs** allow your programs to interact with external data and services, fetching information for you to use.

- **HTTP Requests**: We use the requests library to send HTTP requests to fetch data from APIs.

- **JSON** is the most common data format returned by APIs, and Python's json module makes it easy to parse.

- **Building Apps**: We used a real-world example—building a weather app—to demonstrate how to interact with an API and display the fetched data.

Chapter 11: Database Operations with SQL and Python

What You'll Need

Before diving into database operations, let's make sure you have everything you need to follow along:

1. **A Computer**: Python runs on all major operating systems, including Windows, macOS, and Linux.

2. **Python Installed**: Ensure that Python 3.x is installed. You can download it from python.org.

3. **Libraries**:

   o **SQLite3**: SQLite is a C-language library that provides a lightweight, disk-based database. Python's standard library includes the sqlite3 module, which allows Python to interact with SQLite databases.

   o **SQLAlchemy** (optional): A SQL toolkit and Object-Relational Mapping (ORM) library for Python, though we will focus on SQLite and sqlite3 for this chapter.

You don't need to install SQLite as it's included with Python by default. However, if you'd like to use **SQLAlchemy**, you can install it via:

bash

Once everything is set up, you're ready to start learning and working with databases!

Introduction to Databases and SQL

What is a Database?

A **database** is an organized collection of data that can be easily accessed, managed, and updated. Databases are used in many applications—from web applications and data analysis tools to enterprise software. The data is stored in a structured format and can be queried (searched, retrieved, updated, etc.).

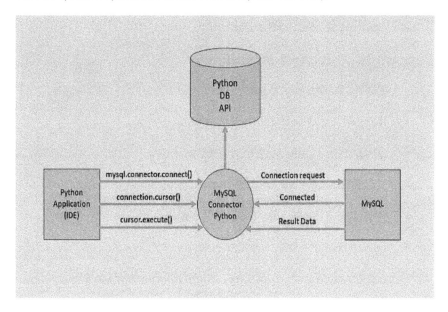

Databases are generally categorized into two types:

- **Relational Databases (RDBMS)**: These use **tables** (rows and columns) to store data, and the data is often queried using

SQL (Structured Query Language). Examples: MySQL, PostgreSQL, SQLite.

- **NoSQL Databases**: These do not use a relational structure and are more flexible in terms of how data is stored. Examples: MongoDB, Cassandra.

What is SQL?

SQL (Structured Query Language) is a standardized programming language used to manage relational databases. SQL allows you to interact with the database by writing queries to:

- Create, read, update, and delete (CRUD) data.

- Define and modify the structure of the database.

- Control access to the data.

Common SQL commands include:

- **SELECT**: Retrieve data from the database.

- **INSERT**: Add data to the database.

- **UPDATE**: Modify data in the database.

- **DELETE**: Remove data from the database.

- **CREATE**: Create new tables or databases.

- **DROP**: Delete tables or databases.

In this chapter, we will use **SQLite**, a lightweight relational database, to interact with data through Python.

1. Working with SQLite

SQLite is a self-contained, serverless, and zero-configuration database engine. It is an excellent choice for small to medium-sized applications or for developers who need a simple database solution without the overhead of setting up and maintaining a server.

1.1 Setting Up SQLite in Python

Python comes with built-in support for SQLite through the sqlite3 module. This means you don't need to install anything extra—SQLite is already available.

Example 1: Connecting to a Database

Let's start by connecting to a database using Python's sqlite3 module. If the database doesn't exist, SQLite will create it automatically.

```python
import sqlite3

# Connect to a SQLite database (it will create the database file if it doesn't exist)
conn = sqlite3.connect('example.db')

# Create a cursor object to interact with the database
cursor = conn.cursor()

# Close the connection (important to always close the connection when done)
conn.close()
```

Explanation:

- sqlite3.connect('example.db') connects to the example.db SQLite database (or creates it if it doesn't exist).

- conn.cursor() creates a cursor object, which allows us to interact with the database.

- conn.close() closes the connection to the database when done.

1.2 Creating Tables

Once connected to the database, you can create tables to store data. A table consists of rows and columns, where each row represents a record, and each column represents an attribute.

Example 2: Creating a Table

Let's create a table to store information about users (e.g., name, age, and email).

```python

import sqlite3

# Connect to the database
conn = sqlite3.connect('example.db')
cursor = conn.cursor()

# Create a new table
cursor.execute('''
CREATE TABLE IF NOT EXISTS users (
    id INTEGER PRIMARY KEY,
```

```
    name TEXT NOT NULL,
    age INTEGER,
    email TEXT
)
""")

# Commit the changes and close the connection
conn.commit()
conn.close()

print("Table created successfully!")
```

Explanation:

- The CREATE TABLE IF NOT EXISTS statement creates a new table called users with four columns: id, name, age, and email.

- id is an integer that serves as the primary key (a unique identifier for each record).

- conn.commit() saves the changes to the database.

- conn.close() closes the connection.

1.3 Inserting Data into a Table

Once you've created a table, you can start adding data to it. You use the INSERT INTO statement to insert new records.

Example 3: Inserting Data

Let's insert a few user records into the users table.

```python
```

```python
import sqlite3

# Connect to the database
conn = sqlite3.connect('example.db')
cursor = conn.cursor()

# Insert some data into the users table
cursor.execute('''
INSERT INTO users (name, age, email)
VALUES ('Alice', 30, 'alice@example.com')
''')
cursor.execute('''
INSERT INTO users (name, age, email)
VALUES ('Bob', 25, 'bob@example.com')
''')

# Commit the changes and close the connection
conn.commit()
conn.close()

print("Data inserted successfully!")
```

Explanation:

- The INSERT INTO statement inserts a new record into the users table. We provide the column names and corresponding values in the VALUES clause.

- conn.commit() saves the changes to the database.

2. Executing Queries with Python

After you have created a table and inserted data, you can retrieve and manipulate the data using SQL queries. In Python, you can execute SQL queries through the cursor object.

2.1 Querying Data from a Table

To fetch data from a table, you use the SELECT statement.

Example 4: Selecting Data

Let's query the users table to retrieve all users' data.

```python
import sqlite3

# Connect to the database
conn = sqlite3.connect('example.db')
cursor = conn.cursor()

# Select all users from the users table
cursor.execute('SELECT * FROM users')

# Fetch all the results
users = cursor.fetchall()

# Display the results
for user in users:
    print(user)
```

```
# Close the connection
conn.close()
```

Explanation:

- cursor.execute('SELECT * FROM users') retrieves all rows from the users table.

- cursor.fetchall() fetches all the results and returns them as a list of tuples.

- Each tuple represents a row in the table, and each item in the tuple corresponds to a column in that row.

2.2 Filtering Data with WHERE Clause

You can filter the data using the WHERE clause to specify conditions.

Example 5: Filtering Data

Let's retrieve users who are older than 30 years.

Explanation:

WHERE age > 30 filters the results to only include users who are older than 30.

2.3 Updating Data

You can update existing records in a table using the UPDATE statement.

Example 6: Updating Data

Let's update Bob's age in the users table.

python

```python
import sqlite3

# Connect to the database
conn = sqlite3.connect('example.db')
cursor = conn.cursor()

# Update Bob's age
cursor.execute('''
UPDATE users
SET age = 26
WHERE name = 'Bob'
''')

# Commit the changes and close the connection
conn.commit()
conn.close()

print("Data updated successfully!")
```

Explanation:

- The UPDATE statement modifies the data in the users table. We set Bob's age to 26 where his name is "Bob".

2.4 Deleting Data

You can delete records from a table using the DELETE statement.

Example 7: Deleting Data

Let's delete Alice's record from the users table.

```python
python python
```

```python
import sqlite3

# Connect to the database
conn = sqlite3.connect('example.db')
cursor = conn.cursor()

# Select users who are older than 30
cursor.execute('SELECT * FROM users WHERE age > 30')

# Fetch all the results
users = cursor.fetchall()

# Display the results
for user in users:
    print(user)

# Close the connection
conn.close()



import sqlite3

# Connect to the database
conn = sqlite3.connect('example.db')
cursor = conn.cursor()

# Delete Alice's record
cursor.execute('''
DELETE FROM users WHERE name = 'Alice'
```

```
""")

# Commit the changes and close the connection
conn.commit()
conn.close()

print("Data deleted successfully!")
```

Explanation:

- The DELETE statement removes records that match the specified condition—in this case, deleting the user with the name "Alice".

---

3. Connecting Python to Databases and Executing Queries

Now that we've covered the basics of SQLite, let's look at how to integrate Python and SQL to automate tasks and execute queries. For example, you could automate the process of storing new user data or fetching records based on specific conditions.

Example 8: Automated User Data Insertion

Let's build a simple Python script that allows users to enter their data and store it in the database.

```python
import sqlite3

def insert_user(name, age, email):
    conn = sqlite3.connect('example.db')
```

```
cursor = conn.cursor()

cursor.execute('''
INSERT INTO users (name, age, email)
VALUES (?, ?, ?)
''', (name, age, email))  # Using placeholders to prevent SQL injection

conn.commit()
conn.close()
print(f"User {name} added successfully!")

# Get user input and insert into the database
name = input("Enter name: ")
age = int(input("Enter age: "))
email = input("Enter email: ")

insert_user(name, age, email)
```

Explanation:

- This script defines a function insert_user() to insert user data into the users table. We use placeholders (?) to prevent **SQL injection** and securely insert the data.

- We prompt the user for their information and then call insert_user() to store the data.

Key Takeaways

- **SQLite** is a simple and lightweight relational database that is built into Python, making it easy to start working with databases.

- **SQL** is the language used to interact with databases, allowing you to **select**, **insert**, **update**, and **delete** data.

- Python's sqlite3 module enables you to connect to SQLite databases, execute SQL queries, and handle data.

- You can automate database tasks such as inserting, querying, and updating data using Python.

Chapter 12: Web Scraping: Extracting Data from Websites

What You'll Need

Before we dive into the exciting world of web scraping, let's make sure you're set up with the necessary tools:

1. **A Computer**: Python runs on all major operating systems: Windows, macOS, and Linux.

2. **Python Installed**: Ensure you have Python 3.x installed. You can download it from python.org.

3. **Libraries**:

   o **requests**: This library allows you to send HTTP requests and get the HTML content of a webpage.

   o **BeautifulSoup**: This library is used to parse HTML and XML documents, making it easy to extract useful data from them.

   o **pandas** (optional, for storing data in CSV): A powerful data manipulation library in Python.

To install the necessary libraries, run the following commands in your terminal/command prompt:

bash

```
pip install requests beautifulsoup4 pandas
```

Once everything is set up, you're ready to start scraping!

Introduction to Web Scraping

Web scraping is the process of extracting data from websites. The data on websites is usually presented in a human-readable format (HTML), but to automate the process of gathering it, we need to "scrape" or extract the data programmatically.

You can scrape a variety of data, such as:

- Product details from e-commerce websites.

- Stock prices from financial websites.

- Weather data from meteorological websites.

- Blog posts or news articles from media websites.

Scraping helps automate the data collection process and allows us to work with the data programmatically. Python, with libraries like **requests** and **BeautifulSoup**, makes it easy to scrape data from websites.

---

1. Basics of Web Scraping

Before starting with Python code, it's important to understand the basic flow of web scraping:

1. **Send an HTTP request** to the website to get the page content.

2. **Parse the HTML content** of the page to extract the data.

3. **Store the extracted data** in a usable format (CSV, database, JSON, etc.).

1.1 Understanding HTML Structure

To effectively scrape data from a website, you need to understand how the data is structured in the page's **HTML** source code. HTML is made up of tags, which can be nested to form a document structure. Common tags you'll encounter are:

- <div>: A generic container used for grouping elements.

- <p>: A paragraph tag, used to display text.

- <a>: A link tag, used for hyperlinks.

- <h1>, <h2>, etc.: Header tags for titles and subheadings.

- <table>, <tr>, <td>: Tags for creating tables and rows.

To get data from a webpage, you need to locate the elements you're interested in, such as titles, images, or prices, and extract them.

---

2. Using BeautifulSoup and Requests

Now that we understand the basics, let's start coding! We'll use **Requests** to fetch the page content and **BeautifulSoup** to parse and extract the data.

2.1 Sending HTTP Requests with Requests

The first step in web scraping is to send a request to the website's server. This is done using the requests library, which is simple and easy to use.

Example 1: Sending a GET Request

```python
import requests

# Define the URL of the website to scrape
url = "https://quotes.toscrape.com/"

# Send a GET request to fetch the HTML content of the page
response = requests.get(url)

# Print the HTML content of the page
print(response.text)
```

Explanation:

- requests.get(url) sends an HTTP GET request to the specified URL.

- response.text contains the raw HTML of the webpage, which we can now parse and extract data from.

2.2 Parsing HTML with BeautifulSoup

Once we have the HTML content, we need to parse it using **BeautifulSoup** to extract the data we want. BeautifulSoup allows us to navigate and search through the HTML structure easily.

Example 2: Parsing HTML with BeautifulSoup

```python
from bs4 import BeautifulSoup
import requests
```

```
# Define the URL of the website to scrape
url = "https://quotes.toscrape.com/"

# Send a GET request to fetch the HTML content of the page
response = requests.get(url)

# Parse the HTML content using BeautifulSoup
soup = BeautifulSoup(response.text, 'html.parser')

# Print the parsed HTML (optional, for debugging)
print(soup.prettify())
```

Explanation:

- BeautifulSoup(response.text, 'html.parser') creates a BeautifulSoup object that represents the parsed HTML document.

- soup.prettify() prints the HTML in a nicely formatted way to help visualize the document structure.

2.3 Extracting Data from HTML

Now that we've parsed the HTML, we can start extracting the data. BeautifulSoup provides several methods to navigate and search the HTML tree, including:

- **find()**: Finds the first element that matches a given tag.

- **find_all()**: Finds all elements that match a given tag.

- **select()**: Finds elements using CSS selectors.

Example 3: Extracting All Quotes

Let's extract all the quotes on the page from the quote class.

```python
from bs4 import BeautifulSoup
import requests

# Define the URL of the website to scrape
url = "https://quotes.toscrape.com/"

# Send a GET request to fetch the HTML content of the page
response = requests.get(url)

# Parse the HTML content using BeautifulSoup
soup = BeautifulSoup(response.text, 'html.parser')

# Find all quote elements
quotes = soup.find_all('span', class_='text')

# Print all the quotes
for quote in quotes:
    print(quote.get_text())
```

Explanation:

- soup.find_all('span', class_='text') finds all <span> elements with the class text (which contain the quotes).

- quote.get_text() extracts the text from each quote tag.

3. Scraping and Storing Data in CSV Files

Now that we know how to extract data from websites, let's look at how to store this data in a CSV file, which is a common format for data storage.

3.1 Introduction to CSV Files

A **CSV (Comma-Separated Values)** file is a simple text file used to store data in a tabular format. Each line represents a row of data, and each value is separated by a comma.

Python's **csv** module makes it easy to read from and write to CSV files.

3.2 Storing Scraped Data in CSV

Let's extend the previous example and store the quotes in a CSV file.

Example 4: Storing Quotes in a CSV File

```python
import csv
from bs4 import BeautifulSoup
import requests

# Define the URL of the website to scrape
url = "https://quotes.toscrape.com/"

# Send a GET request to fetch the HTML content of the page
response = requests.get(url)

# Parse the HTML content using BeautifulSoup
```

```python
soup = BeautifulSoup(response.text, 'html.parser')

# Find all quote elements
quotes = soup.find_all('span', class_='text')

# Open a CSV file to write the data
with open('quotes.csv', mode='w', newline='', encoding='utf-8') as file:
    writer = csv.writer(file)

    # Write the header row
    writer.writerow(['Quote'])

    # Write each quote in the CSV
    for quote in quotes:
        writer.writerow([quote.get_text()])

print("Data has been saved to 'quotes.csv'")
```

Explanation:

- open('quotes.csv', mode='w', newline='', encoding='utf-8') opens a CSV file for writing. If the file doesn't exist, it will be created.

- csv.writer(file) creates a writer object that allows us to write rows of data to the file.

- writer.writerow(['Quote']) writes the header row (column names) to the CSV file.

- The quotes are written row by row using writer.writerow([quote.get_text()]).

4. Real-World Example: Scraping Product Data

Let's apply what we've learned to a real-world example: scraping product data from an e-commerce website.

Imagine you want to scrape the product name, price, and description from a website. We'll use the **example website** http://quotes.toscrape.com/, but in a real-world project, you can use any website with structured data.

Example 5: Scraping Product Data

```python
import csv
from bs4 import BeautifulSoup
import requests

# Define the URL of the e-commerce website
url = "https://quotes.toscrape.com/"

# Send a GET request to fetch the HTML content of the page
response = requests.get(url)

# Parse the HTML content using BeautifulSoup
soup = BeautifulSoup(response.text, 'html.parser')
```

```python
# Find all product containers (replace with actual product container for your website)
product_containers = soup.find_all('div', class_='quote')

# Open a CSV file to write the data
with open('products.csv', mode='w', newline='', encoding='utf-8') as file:
    writer = csv.writer(file)

    # Write the header row
    writer.writerow(['Quote', 'Author', 'Tags'])

    # Write product data to the CSV file
    for container in product_containers:
        quote = container.find('span', class_='text').get_text()
        author = container.find('small', class_='author').get_text()
        tags = [tag.get_text() for tag in container.find_all('a', class_='tag')]

        writer.writerow([quote, author, ", ".join(tags)])

print("Product data has been saved to 'products.csv'")
```

Explanation:

- This script fetches the quotes, authors, and tags from the webpage.

- We iterate over each quote container, extract the relevant data, and store it in a CSV file.

Key Takeaways

- **Web Scraping** is a powerful technique for extracting data from websites and can be applied to various industries like e-commerce, news, and finance.

- **Requests** helps you fetch the HTML content of a webpage.

- **BeautifulSoup** is used to parse the HTML and extract data by searching for specific tags and attributes.

- **CSV Files** are an easy way to store and manipulate scraped data in a tabular format.

- Scraping websites responsibly and following ethical guidelines is crucial. Always check a website's robots.txt file to see if scraping is allowed.

Chapter 13: Machine Learning with Scikit-Learn

What You'll Need

Before we dive into the world of machine learning, let's make sure you have everything set up and ready to go:

1. **A Computer**: Python runs on all major operating systems—Windows, macOS, and Linux.

2. **Python Installed**: Ensure that Python 3.x is installed. You can download the latest version from python.org.

3. **Machine Learning Libraries**: For machine learning in Python, we will use:

   o **Scikit-learn**: A powerful Python library for machine learning, which provides easy-to-use tools for data mining and data analysis.

   o **Pandas**: For data manipulation and analysis.

   o **NumPy**: For numerical operations and handling large datasets.

   o **Matplotlib**: For visualizing data and results.

To install the necessary libraries, run the following command:

bash

```
pip install scikit-learn pandas numpy matplotlib
```

Introduction to Machine Learning Concepts

Machine Learning (ML) is a field of artificial intelligence that enables computers to learn from data and make predictions or decisions without being explicitly programmed for each specific task. In other words, machine learning allows systems to automatically improve their performance on a task based on experience (data).

What is Machine Learning?

Machine learning is all about finding patterns in data. Once we have a model that understands those patterns, we can use it to make predictions on new, unseen data. There are three main types of machine learning:

1. **Supervised Learning**: The model is trained on labeled data (i.e., input data with corresponding output labels). It learns to map inputs to the correct output. Common tasks include classification (e.g., spam detection) and regression (e.g., predicting house prices).

2. **Unsupervised Learning**: The model is trained on unlabeled data. It finds patterns and structures in the data without predefined output labels. Clustering and dimensionality reduction are common tasks.

3. **Reinforcement Learning**: The model learns by interacting with an environment and receiving feedback through rewards or penalties.

For this chapter, we will focus on **Supervised Learning**, specifically using **Linear Regression** to predict continuous values (a common regression task).

1. Implementing Linear Regression with Scikit-Learn

Linear Regression is one of the simplest and most widely used machine learning algorithms. It predicts a continuous output based on one or more input features. It works by fitting a line (or hyperplane in higher dimensions) that best represents the relationship between the input variables (features) and the output variable.

1.1 Understanding the Linear Regression Model

In linear regression, the relationship between the independent variables XXX and the dependent variable yyy is assumed to be linear. Mathematically, this is represented as:

$$y = \beta_0 + \beta_1 \cdot X_1 + \beta_2 \cdot X_2 + \cdots + \beta_n \cdot X_n$$

Where:

- y is the predicted value (dependent variable).

- $X_1, X_2, \dots, X_n$ are the input features (independent variables).

- β_0 is the intercept.

- $\beta_1, \beta_2, \dots, \beta_n$ are the coefficients (weights) that represent the relationship between each feature and the target variable.

1.2 Working with a Simple Linear Regression Example

Let's walk through an example where we predict house prices based on the size of the house (square footage). We'll use the **Boston Housing Dataset**, which is commonly used for regression tasks.

Step 1: Importing the Libraries

python

```python
import numpy as np
import pandas as pd
import matplotlib.pyplot as plt
from sklearn.datasets import load_boston
from sklearn.model_selection import train_test_split
from sklearn.linear_model import LinearRegression
from sklearn.metrics import mean_squared_error, r2_score
```

Explanation:

- load_boston() loads the Boston Housing dataset, which contains features like the size of the house, number of rooms, and the median value of houses in various Boston suburbs.

- train_test_split() will help us split the data into training and testing sets.

Step 2: Loading the Dataset

python

```python
# Load the Boston Housing dataset
boston = load_boston()

# Convert the dataset to a pandas DataFrame for easier handling
df = pd.DataFrame(boston.data, columns=boston.feature_names)
df['PRICE'] = boston.target  # Add target variable (house price)
```

```
# Display the first few rows of the dataset
print(df.head())
```

Explanation:

- We load the Boston dataset and convert it to a pandas DataFrame.

- The target variable (PRICE) is the house price, and the features are the various columns (e.g., the number of rooms, crime rate).

Step 3: Splitting the Data

Next, we split the dataset into a training set (to train the model) and a testing set (to evaluate the model's performance).

python

```
# Features and target
X = df.drop('PRICE', axis=1) # Features (independent variables)
y = df['PRICE'] # Target variable (dependent variable)

# Split the data into training and testing sets
X_train, X_test, y_train, y_test = train_test_split(X, y, test_size=0.2, random_state=42)
```

Explanation:

- X_train, X_test: Features for training and testing.

- y_train, y_test: Target variable (house prices) for training and testing.

- train_test_split() splits the data randomly, with 80% for training and 20% for testing.

Step 4: Creating and Training the Model

Now, we create a **LinearRegression** model and train it on the training data.

python

```python
# Create a Linear Regression model
model = LinearRegression()

# Train the model using the training data
model.fit(X_train, y_train)
```

Explanation:

- model.fit() trains the linear regression model using the training data (X_train and y_train).

Step 5: Making Predictions

Now that we have trained the model, we can use it to make predictions on the testing data.

python

```python
# Make predictions on the test data
y_pred = model.predict(X_test)
```

Explanation:

- model.predict() makes predictions using the trained model on the testing data (X_test).

Step 6: Evaluating the Model

To assess how well our model is performing, we can calculate the **mean squared error** (MSE) and the **R-squared** score.

```python

# Calculate the Mean Squared Error (MSE)
mse = mean_squared_error(y_test, y_pred)
print(f"Mean Squared Error: {mse}")

# Calculate the R-squared score
r2 = r2_score(y_test, y_pred)
print(f"R-squared: {r2}")
```

Explanation:

- The **MSE** tells us how close the predicted values are to the actual values (lower is better).

- The **R-squared** score gives us an indication of how well the model explains the variance in the target variable (a value between 0 and 1, where 1 indicates perfect prediction).

Step 7: Visualizing the Results

Let's visualize the predicted vs actual values on a scatter plot to see how well the model performed.

```python

# Plotting the predicted vs actual values
plt.scatter(y_test, y_pred)
plt.xlabel('Actual Prices')
plt.ylabel('Predicted Prices')
```

plt.title('Actual vs Predicted House Prices')

plt.show()

Explanation:

- This scatter plot will show how well the predicted values match the actual values. Ideally, the points should be close to a straight line.

---

2. Evaluating Machine Learning Models

Evaluating machine learning models is essential to ensure that they are performing well and making accurate predictions. In this section, we will explore how to evaluate machine learning models effectively.

2.1 Performance Metrics for Regression Models

For regression tasks, common performance metrics include:

1. **Mean Squared Error (MSE)**: Measures the average squared difference between predicted and actual values. A lower MSE indicates better model performance.

2. **R-squared (R^2)**: Represents the proportion of variance in the dependent variable explained by the model. A higher R^2 indicates better model performance.

3. **Root Mean Squared Error (RMSE)**: The square root of MSE, which gives the error in the same units as the target variable.

2.2 Cross-Validation

Cross-validation is a technique to assess how the model generalizes to an independent dataset. It involves splitting the data into multiple subsets and training and testing the model on different combinations of these subsets.

Example 8: Cross-Validation in Scikit-Learn

```python
from sklearn.model_selection import cross_val_score

# Perform 5-fold cross-validation
cv_scores = cross_val_score(model, X, y, cv=5)

# Print the cross-validation scores
print(f"Cross-validation scores: {cv_scores}")
print(f"Mean cross-validation score: {cv_scores.mean()}")
```

Explanation:

- cross_val_score() performs cross-validation on the dataset, returning an array of scores for each fold.

- The mean of these scores gives us an overall performance metric for the model.

2.3 Hyperparameter Tuning

Many machine learning models, including linear regression, have hyperparameters that can affect their performance. In the case of **Linear Regression,** we can tune the regularization strength (if using techniques like Ridge or Lasso regression).

Example 9: Tuning Ridge Regression

```python
from sklearn.linear_model import Ridge

# Create a Ridge Regression model with a regularization parameter
```

```
ridge_model = Ridge(alpha=1.0)

# Train the model
ridge_model.fit(X_train, y_train)

# Make predictions and evaluate
ridge_y_pred = ridge_model.predict(X_test)
ridge_mse = mean_squared_error(y_test, ridge_y_pred)
print(f"Ridge Regression MSE: {ridge_mse}")
```

Explanation:

- The alpha parameter in Ridge regression controls the strength of the regularization. A higher alpha value results in stronger regularization.

Key Takeaways

- **Machine Learning** allows computers to learn patterns from data and make predictions or decisions without being explicitly programmed.

- **Linear Regression** is a simple yet powerful model for predicting continuous values based on input features.

- **Scikit-learn** provides easy-to-use tools for creating machine learning models, evaluating their performance, and tuning them for optimal results.

- **Evaluating Models** using metrics like Mean Squared Error (MSE) and R-squared (R^2) helps assess how well the model performs.

- **Cross-Validation** and **Hyperparameter Tuning** are essential steps in improving model performance.

Chapter 14: Building a Python-Powered E-Commerce Application

What You'll Need

Before you dive into building an e-commerce application with Python, let's make sure you have everything in place to follow along:

1. **A Computer**: Python works on all major operating systems (Windows, macOS, Linux).

2. **Python Installed**: Ensure that Python 3.x is installed. You can download it from python.org.

3. **Required Libraries**:

   o **Flask**: A web framework for building web applications in Python.

   o **SQLite**: A lightweight database engine for managing our application data.

   o **Jinja2**: The templating engine that comes with Flask to render dynamic HTML.

   o **WTForms**: A library for creating forms in Flask applications.

   o **Flask-Login**: A Flask extension for managing user authentication.

To install the necessary libraries, you can run:

bash

```
pip install flask sqlite3 flask-login flask-wtf
```

Once you have these installed, you're ready to start building your e-commerce application!

Introduction to Building E-Commerce Applications

Building an e-commerce application involves creating a platform where users can browse products, add them to a shopping cart, and make purchases. An e-commerce site has both **front-end** and **back-end** components that need to work together seamlessly to provide a smooth user experience.

In this chapter, we will:

1. Plan and design the structure of our e-commerce site.

2. Set up the **front-end** using HTML, CSS, and **Jinja2** templates.

3. Implement the **back-end** logic with Flask, including handling product data and user authentication.

4. Manage user accounts and order data with a database.

Let's break it down step by step.

1. Planning and Designing an E-Commerce Site

Before jumping into code, it's crucial to plan and design your application. Let's focus on the core features and functionality that every e-commerce site needs:

1.1 Core Features of an E-Commerce Site

1. **Product Listings**: Display products with details like name, price, description, and images.

2. **Product Categories**: Organize products into categories for easier navigation.

3. **Shopping Cart**: Let users add and remove products from their cart before checkout.

4. **User Authentication**: Allow users to register, log in, and manage their accounts.

5. **Order Management**: Enable users to place orders and view their order history.

1.2 Database Design

For an e-commerce application, we need to store data such as products, users, and orders. A simple relational database using **SQLite** will work well for this example.

Tables in the Database:

1. **Users**: Store user information such as name, email, and password.

2. **Products**: Store product details like name, description, price, and stock.

3. **Orders**: Store details of customer orders, such as products purchased, quantities, and total price.

4. **Shopping Cart**: Temporarily store items a user adds to their cart before checkout.

---

2. Integrating Front-End and Back-End with Flask

Flask will serve as the **back-end** framework, handling the logic of product management, user authentication, and order processing. The **front-end** will be built using HTML and CSS, with **Jinja2** templates to render dynamic content.

2.1 Setting Up Flask Application

Let's create the basic structure for our Flask application.

Step 1: Create a Flask Project

1. **Project Structure**:

```php
ecommerce-app/
│
├── app.py          # Main application file
├── templates/      # HTML templates for the front-end
│   ├── base.html   # Base template (common layout)
│   ├── index.html  # Homepage
│   ├── product.html # Product detail page
│   └── cart.html   # Shopping cart page
│
```

```
├── static/         # CSS, images, and other static files
│    └── style.css   # Stylesheet for the application
│
├── database.db      # SQLite database
└── requirements.txt # File for listing Python dependencies
```

Step 2: Initialize Flask App

In your app.py, import Flask and initialize the app:

```python
from flask import Flask, render_template, redirect, url_for
from flask_sqlalchemy import SQLAlchemy
from flask_login import LoginManager

app = Flask(__name__)
app.config['SECRET_KEY'] = 'your_secret_key'
app.config['SQLALCHEMY_DATABASE_URI'] = 'sqlite:///database.db'

# Initialize the database
db = SQLAlchemy(app)

# Initialize login manager
login_manager = LoginManager(app)
login_manager.login_view = 'login'

if __name__ == '__main__':
    app.run(debug=True)
```

Explanation:

- **SQLAlchemy** handles the database operations.

- **LoginManager** manages user sessions for authentication.

2.2 Creating Templates with Jinja2

Flask uses **Jinja2** as its templating engine. With Jinja2, you can create dynamic HTML pages by embedding Python code within your HTML.

Step 3: Base Template (base.html)

Create a base template that includes common elements like the header, footer, and navigation bar.

```
html

<!DOCTYPE html>
<html lang="en">
<head>
    <meta charset="UTF-8">
    <meta name="viewport" content="width=device-width, initial-scale=1.0">
    <title>E-Commerce App</title>
    <link rel="stylesheet" href="{{ url_for('static', filename='style.css') }}">
</head>
<body>
    <header>
        <nav>
            <a href="{{ url_for('home') }}">Home</a>
            <a href="{{ url_for('cart') }}">Cart</a>
            {% if current_user.is_authenticated %}
                <a href="{{ url_for('logout') }}">Logout</a>
            {% else %}
```

```
        <a href="{{ url_for('login') }}">Login</a>
      {% endif %}
    </nav>
  </header>

  {% block content %}
  {% endblock %}
</body>
</html>
```

Explanation:

- {{ url_for('home') }} dynamically generates the URL for the homepage.

- {% block content %} is where the page-specific content will go.

Step 4: Homepage Template (index.html)

Create a homepage that displays a list of products.

```html

{% extends 'base.html' %}

{% block content %}
<h1>Welcome to Our E-Commerce Site</h1>
<div class="products">
  {% for product in products %}
  <div class="product">
    <h2>{{ product.name }}</h2>
```

```
<p>{{ product.description }}</p>
<p>${{ product.price }}</p>
<a href="{{ url_for('view_product', product_id=product.id) }}">View
Product</a>
</div>
{% endfor %}
</div>
{% endblock %}
```

Explanation:

- {% for product in products %} loops through the list of products and displays each one.

- {{ url_for('view_product', product_id=product.id) }} creates a link to the product's detail page.

2.3 Connecting to the Database

Create models for users and products using **SQLAlchemy**.

Step 5: Define Models

In app.py, define models for **User** and **Product**.

```python
class User(db.Model):
    id = db.Column(db.Integer, primary_key=True)
    username = db.Column(db.String(100), unique=True, nullable=False)
    password = db.Column(db.String(100), nullable=False)

class Product(db.Model):
    id = db.Column(db.Integer, primary_key=True)
    name = db.Column(db.String(100), nullable=False)
```

```
description = db.Column(db.String(500), nullable=False)
price = db.Column(db.Float, nullable=False)
```

Explanation:

- User and Product classes are defined with fields that represent the columns in their respective tables.

- db.Column() specifies the type and constraints (e.g., nullable=False means the field cannot be empty).

Step 6: Creating the Database

Run the following Python code to create the tables in the database:

```python
from app import db

# Create the tables
db.create_all()
```

3. User Authentication and Database Management

Now that we have the basic structure set up, let's implement user authentication and handle product data.

3.1 User Registration and Login

Using **Flask-Login**, we can easily manage user authentication. We'll create a registration form, login form, and logout functionality.

Step 7: User Registration Form

Create a simple registration form in register.html.

```
html
```

```
{% extends 'base.html' %}

{% block content %}
<h1>Register</h1>
<form method="POST">
    <label for="username">Username</label>
    <input type="text" name="username" required>
    <label for="password">Password</label>
    <input type="password" name="password" required>
    <button type="submit">Register</button>
</form>
{% endblock %}
```

Step 8: Registering Users

In app.py, create the route to handle user registration.

```
python
```

```python
from flask import render_template, redirect, url_for, request
from flask_login import login_user

@app.route('/register', methods=['GET', 'POST'])
def register():
    if request.method == 'POST':
        username = request.form['username']
        password = request.form['password']
        user = User(username=username, password=password)
        db.session.add(user)
```

```
db.session.commit()
login_user(user)
return redirect(url_for('home'))
return render_template('register.html')
```

Explanation:

- When the form is submitted (POST), we create a new User object and save it to the database.

- login_user(user) logs the user in immediately after registration.

4. Wrapping Up: E-Commerce Features

At this point, you've set up the basics of an e-commerce application. The next steps are:

- Adding product categories.

- Implementing a shopping cart.

- Allowing users to place orders.

- Implementing an admin interface to manage products.

Key Takeaways

- **Flask** is an excellent framework for building web applications, including e-commerce sites.

- **SQLite** and **SQLAlchemy** provide a simple yet powerful way to store and manage data.

- **Jinja2** allows us to dynamically render HTML pages, making the front-end part of the e-commerce site flexible and user-friendly.

- **Flask-Login** provides easy authentication, allowing users to register, log in, and manage their accounts securely.

Chapter 15: Capstone Project: Building a Complete Python Application

What You'll Need

Before we begin building our Python application, let's ensure you have everything in place:

1. **A Computer**: Python can be run on all major operating systems: Windows, macOS, and Linux.

2. **Python Installed**: Ensure that Python 3.x is installed on your computer. You can download the latest version from python.org.

3. **Libraries and Tools**:

    o   **Flask**: For creating web applications in Python.

    o   **SQLite** or **PostgreSQL** (optional): For managing databases.

    o   **Jinja2**: For templating HTML.

    o   **Bootstrap**: For styling the front-end (optional).

    o   **Git**: For version control (optional but recommended).

    o   **Heroku** or **AWS**: For deployment (we will focus on Heroku for simplicity).

To install the necessary libraries, you can run:

```
bash
```

```
pip install flask flask_sqlalchemy
```

Once you have these tools ready, you are all set to begin!

Introduction to the Capstone Project

A **Capstone Project** is the culmination of all the skills you've learned in this book. It's your opportunity to apply what you've studied by developing a fully functional application that can be deployed and used in the real world.

In this chapter, we will guide you through the development of a complete Python application. You will:

1. **Plan and design** the project.

2. **Build the application** using Python and Flask.

3. **Test** the application to ensure it works as expected.

4. **Deploy the application** to a live environment so others can use it.

By the end of this chapter, you will have a real-world project to add to your portfolio, showcasing your skills in full-stack development, database management, and web application deployment.

---

1. Bringing Everything Together

In the previous chapters, you learned various concepts, including web scraping, machine learning, working with databases, and more.

Now, it's time to combine all these skills into a complete Python application.

1.1 Choosing the Project

The first step is to choose the type of application you want to build. Since we've learned about databases, web frameworks, and user authentication, let's create an **E-commerce Store**. This project will involve:

- **Product Listings**: Display products with details like price, description, and images.

- **User Authentication**: Allow users to register, log in, and make purchases.

- **Shopping Cart**: Enable users to add items to their cart.

- **Order Management**: Allow users to place orders and view their order history.

---

2. Step-by-Step Project Development

2.1 Setting Up Flask Application

Start by setting up a basic Flask application. If you don't already have a project structure, here's a simple layout:

```php
ecommerce/
│
├── app.py          # Main application file
├── templates/      # HTML templates for the front-end
│   ├── base.html   # Base template (common layout)
```

```
│   ├── index.html   # Homepage
│   ├── product.html # Product detail page
│   └── cart.html    # Shopping cart page
│
├── static/       # CSS, images, and other static files
│   └── style.css   # Stylesheet for the application
│
├── database.db     # SQLite database
└── requirements.txt # File for listing Python dependencies
```

Example: Basic Flask App Setup

python

```python
from flask import Flask, render_template, request, redirect, url_for
from flask_sqlalchemy import SQLAlchemy

app = Flask(__name__)
app.config['SECRET_KEY'] = 'your_secret_key'
app.config['SQLALCHEMY_DATABASE_URI'] = 'sqlite:///database.db'

# Initialize the database
db = SQLAlchemy(app)

@app.route('/')
def home():
    return render_template('index.html')

if __name__ == '__main__':
    app.run(debug=True)
```

169

Explanation:

- We initialize the Flask app and the database (SQLAlchemy).

- The home() route renders the index.html template.

2.2 Database Models

Now, let's define the models for our application. We will have two main models: **Product** and **User**.

Example: Product and User Models

```python
class Product(db.Model):
    id = db.Column(db.Integer, primary_key=True)
    name = db.Column(db.String(100), nullable=False)
    description = db.Column(db.String(500), nullable=False)
    price = db.Column(db.Float, nullable=False)


class User(db.Model):
    id = db.Column(db.Integer, primary_key=True)
    username = db.Column(db.String(100), unique=True, nullable=False)
    password = db.Column(db.String(100), nullable=False)
```

Explanation:

- Product has id, name, description, and price attributes to store product data.

- User has username and password fields for user authentication.

2.3 Handling User Authentication

User authentication is essential in e-commerce sites. We will use **Flask-Login** to manage user sessions.

Example: User Registration

First, create a form for user registration in register.html:

html

```
<form method="POST" action="{{ url_for('register') }}">
    <label for="username">Username</label>
    <input type="text" name="username" required>
    <label for="password">Password</label>
    <input type="password" name="password" required>
    <button type="submit">Register</button>
</form>
```

Then, create a route in app.py to handle user registration:

python

```
from flask_login import login_user
from werkzeug.security import generate_password_hash

@app.route('/register', methods=['GET', 'POST'])
def register():
    if request.method == 'POST':
        username = request.form['username']
        password = generate_password_hash(request.form['password'])
        new_user = User(username=username, password=password)
        db.session.add(new_user)
        db.session.commit()
```

```
    login_user(new_user)
    return redirect(url_for('home'))
return render_template('register.html')
```

Explanation:

- generate_password_hash() securely hashes the password before storing it.

- login_user() logs the user in automatically after registration.

2.4 Product Listings and Detail Page

Next, create the routes and templates for listing products and viewing product details.

Example: Displaying Products

In the index.html template, loop through the products and display them:

html

```
{% for product in products %}
    <div class="product">
        <h2>{{ product.name }}</h2>
        <p>{{ product.description }}</p>
        <p>${{ product.price }}</p>
        <a href="{{ url_for('view_product', product_id=product.id) }}">View Product</a>
    </div>
{% endfor %}
```

In app.py, query the products from the database and pass them to the template:

python

```python
@app.route('/')
def home():
    products = Product.query.all()
    return render_template('index.html', products=products)
```

Example: Product Detail Page

Create a route to display detailed information about a product.

python

```python
@app.route('/product/<int:product_id>')
def view_product(product_id):
    product = Product.query.get_or_404(product_id)
    return render_template('product.html', product=product)
```

Explanation:

- Product.query.all() retrieves all products.

- Product.query.get_or_404() retrieves a single product by its id, or returns a 404 error if the product is not found.

---

3. Step-by-Step Project Development

3.1 Implementing the Shopping Cart

Now, let's implement a shopping cart where users can add products.

Example: Cart Model

Create a Cart model to store items that a user adds to their cart:

python

```python
class Cart(db.Model):
```

```
id = db.Column(db.Integer, primary_key=True)

user_id = db.Column(db.Integer, db.ForeignKey('user.id'), nullable=False)

product_id = db.Column(db.Integer, db.ForeignKey('product.id'),
nullable=False)

quantity = db.Column(db.Integer, default=1)
```

Example: Adding Products to Cart

Create a route to add products to the cart:

python

```python
@app.route('/add_to_cart/<int:product_id>')
def add_to_cart(product_id):
    product = Product.query.get_or_404(product_id)
    # Add the product to the cart
    cart_item = Cart(user_id=current_user.id, product_id=product.id)
    db.session.add(cart_item)
    db.session.commit()
    return redirect(url_for('cart'))
```

Example: Viewing Cart

Create a route to view the shopping cart:

python

```python
@app.route('/cart')
def cart():
    cart_items = Cart.query.filter_by(user_id=current_user.id).all()
    return render_template('cart.html', cart_items=cart_items)
```

4. Deploying Your Application

After building and testing the application, the next step is deployment. We will deploy the application to **Heroku**, a popular platform for deploying web applications.

4.1 Setting Up Heroku

1. Install **Heroku CLI**: Download and install the Heroku CLI from Heroku's website.

2. **Login to Heroku**: Open your terminal and log in by running heroku login.

4.2 Preparing Your Application for Deployment

1. **Create a Procfile**: This file tells Heroku how to run your app.

```bash
```

```
web: gunicorn app:app
```

Install Gunicorn: Gunicorn is a Python WSGI server for running Flask applications in production.

```bash
```

```
pip install gunicorn
```

Create requirements.txt: This file lists the libraries needed to run your application.

```bash
```

```
pip freeze > requirements.txt
```

4.3 Deploying to Heroku

1. Initialize a Git repository (if you haven't already):

```bash
```

175

```
git init
git add .
git commit -m "Initial commit"
Create a Heroku app:
bash


heroku create my-ecommerce-app
Push the code to Heroku:
bash


git push heroku master
Open the app:
bash


heroku open
```

Key Takeaways

- **Flask** is a powerful web framework that allows you to build web applications quickly and easily.

- **SQLAlchemy** helps you manage your database models and relationships in Flask.

- **Jinja2** templates allow you to render dynamic HTML pages that interact with your database.

- **User authentication** can be managed with **Flask-Login** to keep your application secure.

- **Deployment** to platforms like **Heroku** makes your application accessible to users around the world.

www.ingramcontent.com/pod-product-compliance
Lightning Source LLC
Chambersburg PA
CBHW070949050326
40689CB00014B/3399